JEWISH
CROSSWORD
PUZZLES

JEWISH CROSSWORD PUZZLES

KATHI HANDLER

JASON ARONSON INC.
Northvale, New Jersey
Jerusalem

This book was set in 12 pt. New Baskerville by Alpha Graphics, of Pittsfield, New Hampshire.

International Book Number: 076579988 X

Manufactured in the United States of America. Jason Aronson Inc. offers books and cassettes. For information and catalog write to Jason Aronson Inc., 230 Livingston Street, Northvale, NJ 07647.

Introduction

Hello crossword fans! Nobody loves a leisurely afternoon working a challenging crossword more than I do, but I've noticed that they didn't touch on my Jewishness. So I decided to write crosswords that challenge my Jewish knowledge. Now you can test your Jewish knowledge too! Test your knowledge of Jewish sports, history, *Yiddishkeit*, religion, Israeli geography, and all aspects of Jewish life. If you know the difference between a *chazzer* and a *chazzan*, or a *schlemiel* and a *schlemazal*, then you are in for a real treat.

*To my
loving husband,
Gary*

Puzzles

Puzzle 1

Across

1. Felafel holder
5. Four (Hebrew)
10. Moses' last mount
14. Ibn Gabirol specialty
15. Actress Radner
16. Esther's kingdom
17. Naphtali's mom
18. Hitler
19. Kinneret
20. Jacob after the angel
21. *Tal* (English)
22. H-Bomb scientist
24. *Tuches*
26. Corpse
27. Expire
30. Drill
31. Gaza to Be'er Sheva (dir.)
34. Emulate Abba Eban
35. Moan
36. American Mossad
37. Plague
38. *Schmatah* (English)
39. One of the Stooges
40. __ Man, Doron Sheffer
41. Eilat, old style
42. Pianist Victor
43. Sighs
44. *Mikveh*
45. Like a *Hamantaschen*
46. Wagon
47. Seder salt water
48. Saul's boy
51. Soon
52. *Tallit* hanger
56. *Chazzer* (English)
57. Men from Chelm
59. __ *the Terrible,* Treblinka
60. *The New Colossus* poetess
61. Medad or Eldad
62. *Seraphim* wings?
63. Crest
64. Job's travails
65. *Simcha*

Down

1. Harris stats.
2. Einstein specialty
3. Shamsky's Mets
4. Zilpah's progeny
5. Tales
6. Never on *Shabbat*
7. Sound the shofar
8. Anti-Semitism fighters
9. Bar Mitzvah reading
10. Poetess Sachs
11. Security experts
12. Make the *Challah*
13. Tenth part of an ephah
23. Paradise
25. Haifa to Tiberias (dir.)
26. Sukkah
27. Cured by Salk's vaccine
28. Fromm or Segal
29. Maccabiah activities
30. Jewish penicillin
31. Feeling for Haman
32. Masada event

33. Enjoyed the Seder
35. Super kosher
38. Benny Goodman's instrument
39. Sits *shiva*
41. Orator
42. Gottex suit top
45. Sellers and Lorre
46. Eilat reef

47. Hebrew month
48. Vigoda and Fortas
49. Empire over Israel
50. Zilpah, to Asher
51. Jews (Yiddish)
53. Amalek or Hitler
54. Staff
55. Al Jolson position
58. Purim drink

1	2	3	4	■	5	6	7	8	9	■	10	11	12	13
14				■	15					■	16			
17				■	18					■	19			
20				■	21			■	22	23				
■	■	24	25				■	26				■	■	■
27	28	29				■	30				■	31	32	33
34				■	35					■	36			
37				■	38				■	39				
40			■	41					■	42				
43			■	44			■	45						
■	■	46				■	47				■	■	■	■
48	49	50			■	51			■	52	53	54	55	
56			■	57	58				■	59				
60			■	61					■	62				
63			■	64					■	65				

Puzzle 2

Across

1. Divorce paper
4. *Yeled* (English)
7. Herman Barron need
10. Man of great faith
13. In front of
14. Campaign organization
15. Hirsch to friends
16. Fruit drink
17. Prophet of the return
19. Enjoyed manna
20. Sopher need
21. Noah's boat
22. Jacob's mother
25. Israeli Presidential term
27. Folk guitarist Bob
28. Chant Torah
31. Son of Gad
32. Villain
33. "__Pass" (Uris)
34. Close of *Shabbat*
36. Squashed
37. Garden

38. Rachel to Joseph
39. *Shin Bet*
42. Sealed with a *Ketubah*
46. Toting an Uzi
47. *Hora*
48. Moses' aura
49. *Tuches*
50. Two old shekels
51. Bris must
52. Israeli flag feature
54. Salk's milieu
55. *Vav* with a dot
57. Jewish organization
58. Masada finale
62. Gaza to Jerusalem (dir.)
63. Last degree
64. Haifa to Tiberias (dir.)
65. Canasta card
66. "Gingy"
67. Sighs
68. Owns
69. *Bubkes*

Down

1. Eilat stone
2. B.C.E. word
3. Coastal city
4. Hamsa hope
5. Abraham J. Heschel
6. Tevye
7. Minister of immigration
8. Adam's apple
9. Valley (Hebrew)
10. Noah's son
11. Nelly Sachs specialty

12. Cardozo to friends
18. Exist
23. Israeli Valley
24. Haman's eighth
25. Yiddish disdain
26. Songwriter Gershwin
27. Fourth letter of *Alephbet*
29. Purim drink
30. Adam to Seth
32. Edomite king
33. Book by M. Buber

35. *Negev*
36. *Tsahal* drill
38. Ephraim's brother
39. Deface
40. Solomon's mine find
41. Windows on Kristalnacht
42. Create
43. Ishmael progeny
44. Olympian Friedman
45. Evil__

47. Deeps
50. Occasion for a bris
51. Apple computer
53. Barrett
54. Breaks the ninth
55. Over to Bialik
56. *Shema* ender
59. Lands of the Covenant
60. 601
61. Wiggling *treif* fish

Puzzle 3

Across

1. Robinson and Cantor
4. Equipment for Chagall
10. Eden exile
14. Reason for *shiva*
15. Moses' bush
16. The strip
17. Jacob's boy
18. Bargain basement brother
19. Alephbet member
20. Night before
22. Scream
23. Internal Revenue Service (abbr.)
24. Israeli neighbors
26. Passover
29. 100 *agarot*
30. Monty Hall specialty
31. Old woman
33. Offered by Lenders
36. __ after meals
37. Solomon's find
38. Gabbai catch
39. Fromm or Segal
40. *Hatikvah, The* __
41. Herman Barron need
42. Moses on the mount
43. Gabriel and Uriel headgear
44. *Shikker*'s choice
45. Purim garb
46. Baseball's Gordon
47. Comedian Marty
49. Woody Allen film
53. Ancient deity figure
54. *Lamed* (English)
55. Arrow
56. Abraham to Ishmael
58. Deli fare
61. Business degree
62. Month before Nisan
63. Israeli coins
64. *Ess* (English)
65. *Shiva* clothes
66. High priests?
67. Her

Down

1. *Tsitsit* site
2. Anne's book
3. Nisan feast
4. *Fay* (English)
5. Non-Hebrew tribes
6. Comic Soupy
7. Valley (Hebrew)
8. Nimoy casually
9. Haifa to Hebron (dir.)
10. 100th of an NIS
11. Schechter institution
12. B'nai B'rith youth organization
13. Adam was the first
21. Kedem needs
23. Ellis
25. Named in a *Mishaberach*
26. Shalom
27. Apiece
28. Mute Marx
30. After *Kiddush*
32. *Gimels* (English)

33. Zeta __ Tau, fraternity
34. Son of Gad
35. Federal Reserve chairman
36. Artist Chaim
39. On high (Hebrew)
40. Son of Ishmael
42. Ender
43. Biblical measure
46. Lox
48. *Bigthan* or *Teresh*

49. Sound the shofar
50. Items on Schindler's list
51. Four (Hebrew)
52. Israel in 1948
54. King of Israel
56. Amy Alcott's score
57. Fruit drink
58. Pouch
59. Before
60. Tis, to Nelly Sachs

Puzzle 4

Across

1. Dike
4. Houdini specialty
10. Lot's wife
14. Son of Gad
15. Kosher fish features
16. 2,002
17. Kunstler organization
18. Scrolls
19. Cleo killers
20. Seder shank
22. Vase
23. Imitate Goldie Hawn
24. Yom Kippur condition
26. Branded like Cain
29. Sighs
30. Actress Theda
31. Act the *gonif*
33. __ *Hall*, Allen film
36. Masada sport
37. *Daled* (English)
38. Phyllis Diller volume
39. Oasis appeal
40. Wagon
41. Arkia milieu
42. *Hamantasch* filling
43. Amulet
44. Haifa to Hebron (dir.)
45. *Agadah*
46. Pouch
47. Preserve
49. Rebuild the Temple
53. *Tuches*
54. "Sea" to Chagall
55. Esther's kingdom
56. Eve's son
58. Israel neighbor
61. Acted
62. Actor Reiner
63. Like Dachau wire
64. Gaza to Eilat (dir.)
65. Roasted on *Pesach*
66. Lox companion
67. Knicks coach, Holzman

Down

1. Played canasta
2. Four (Hebrew)
3. Where Bubbe went
4. Hester Street time zone
5. Caleb and Joshua
6. Not on *Shabbas*
7. Arkin or King
8. Alephbet member
9. Eat (Yiddish)
10. *Potch* (English)
11. Anne Frank's home
12. Rim
13. It is, to Ha-Levi
21. *Havdalah* candle
23. PLO member
25. Her
26. Zilpah and Bilhah
27. *Tsahal*
28. *Machers*
30. Tool for the Mohel
32. Zeta __ Tau, fraternity
33. Sigh

34. Grogger emanation
35. War crimes trials
36. Naive shtetl
39. Crest
40. Sabras
42. Musician Getz
43. Owns
46. World for Koufax
48. Male cattle
49. The Lubavitcher

50. Seder
51. *Hagba'ah*
52. Said Amen
54. Messiah mount
56. Canasta card
57. Scrip
58. Alphabet run
59. Cheer
60. Fruit drink

Puzzle 5

Across

1. Make *aliyah*
5. Seventh king
9. Solomon
13. Lauder
15. Songwriter Simon
16. Magic Carpet source
17. Like Samson's hair
18. Felafel holder
20. __ *Crowd*, Birmingham novel
21. Acre to Tiberias (dir.)
23. E. Lazarus specialty
24. Capp and Jolson
25. Isaac stand-in
26. Seder
28. Number ending
30. Thou possessive
31. Ellis and Staten
33. Acted the bigot
37. Golden girl Arthur
38. Tu B' Shevat planting
40. Ache
41. Jerusalem windmill builder
46. ___ *Shabbat*
47. C.E. word
48. Acted
49. Started
51. Life and Knowledge
53. Adam to Seth
56. Hebrew letter
58. *Tsimmes*
59. Exist
60. __ *Promise*, by Potok
63. Hammerin' Hank's tool
65. Her
66. Israeli coin
67. Western Wall tunnel
70. *Hagba'ah*
72. Samson's refuge rock
73. Actor Kaplin
74. Nazarite no no
75. Mayor Olmert
76. Tenth part of an ephah
77. Like *shiva* clothes

Down

1. Ein Gedi
2. Son of Asher
3. Forty day forecast
4. Ever to Bialik
5. UJA word
6. Israeli conquest
7. Paul Newman's hobby
8. Circumcision tool
9. Six days long event
10. Einstein specialty
11. Crest
12. *Tsitsit* site
14. Philistines and Edomites
19. House (Hebrew comb. word)
22. Tahina
27. 1917 United States lightweight boxing champion
29. Lubavitch
32. Used his *tuches*
34. Also

35. Hank Greenberg stat.
36. *Daled* (English)
37. Bore biblically
39. Issachar city
41. Group for Bugsy Siegel
42. *Shema* ender
43. Portion (abbr.)
44. Jewish organization
45. Anglers
50. Jordanian Mount
52. Disney exec.

53. Great prophet
54. Haman's eighth
55. Sinai
57. Arthur Murray step
60. You, biblically
61. Owns, biblically
62. Father of Edomites
64. Koufax club
68. 2,500
69. Heschel, to friends
71. Expressions of ease

1	2	3	4		5	6	7	8		9	10	11	12
13			14		15					16			
17					18			19					
20				21	22			23				24		
25				26			27		28		29			
30				31				32		33		34	35	36
			37				38		39		40			
41	42	43				44				45				
46					47				48					
49				50		51		52				53	54	55
			56		57		58					59		
60	61	62			63		64		65				66	
67			68				69			70	71			
72					73					74				
75					76						77			

Puzzle 6

Across

1. Asner and Koch
4. Singing brothers
7. 1,200
10. *Meshugge* (English)
13. Dues
14. Canasta card
15. Gershwin
16. Hellenistic or Biblical
17. Pita stuffing
19. Karpas ritual
20. Like David from Saul
21. Kosher hooves
22. Rosenbergs?
24. Alphabet run
25. Rickles specialty
27. Owned
28. Not with meat
29. Leather punch
32. The Heights
34. Bob Dylan to 39 across
35. Seventh king
37. __ Crowd, Birmingham novel
38. Literary initials
39. Folk singer and guitarist
45. Israeli coin
46. Exodus egress
47. *Mizrach* location
48. Use your shekels
51. Torah decorations
53. Cheer
54. Uriel's headgear
55. Michael Landon role
56. Bear false witness
58. In front of
59. Evil eye
61. *Schmatah*, at times (English)
65. Hebrew letter
66. Total
67. Singer Barry
69. Fruit drink
70. *Vav* (English)
71. Gives a shank
72. Collection of facts
73. Plagues
74. Hamantaschen
75. *Schlissel* (English)
76. Goldwyn company

Down

1. *Fays* (English)
2. Jonah milieu
3. Barter
4. Plump (Yiddish)
5. __ man, Doron Sheffer
6. Allen and Blanc
7. Abraham's son
8. *Shivah* sounds
9. *Yarmulkes*
10. Levi's third son
11. Israel's neighbor
12. *Horas*
18. Arkia milieu
23. Sadducees opponents
26. *Tsahal* footwear
28. Shofar's sound
29. Ribicoff
30. Which one?

31. Sabin's milieu
33. Bethel?
34. Vote yes
36. Sculptor Elkan
38. K'tonton
40. Got away
41. Brooks
42. Deface
43. Third king of Judah
44. Last degree
48. Hebrew month
49. *Adloyadah*

50. Joseph's brothers
51. Line with Jordan
52. Author Sheldon
55. Land of Judah
57. Son of Gad
59. *Machpelah*
60. Valley (Hebrew)
62. Israelite city
63. Rock of Ages
64. Emulated Spitz
68. Tens days long

1	2	3		4	5	6		7	8	9		10	11	12
13				14				15				16		
17			18					19				20		
21						22	23					24		
			25		26		27				28			
29	30	31		32		33				34				
35			36		37				38					
39				40				41				42	43	44
			45				46				47			
48	49	50				51				52		53		
54					55				56		57			
58				59				60		61		62	63	64
65				66				67	68					
69				70				71				72		
73				74				75				76		

Puzzle 7

Across

1. Tu B' Shevat planting
4. Designer
8. Remembered by *Yahrzeit*
13. Sid Gordon's stat.
14. *Dreidel*
15. Tenth minor prophet
16. Torah breastplate
17. Sigh
18. Gabriel and Uriel
19. Plague
21. Dreidel actions
23. Like Samson's hair
25. Singer Manilow
26. Sculptor's style
29. Emulate Wiesenthal
30. Micah and Nahum
31. Cardozo and Goodman
32. Neither's partner
33. Exodus leader
34. Bandleader Shaw
35. *Meshugge* (English)
37. Israeli resort
39. Expert (Yiddish)
41. Klezmer groups
43. El-Al posting
46. Hebrew letter
47. Dead Sea plenty
48. Tenth part of an ephah
49. Mauri Rose need
50. *The Angry__*, Uris novel
51. *Chazzers* (English)
52. Matzo ball server
53. Einstein
54. Covet
57. Singer Diamond
59. True man of Sodom
62. *Bimahs*
63. Equipment for Koufax
64. Gaza to Jerusalem (dir.)
65. Anne's book
66. Youngman hope
67. "Gingy"

Down

1. Jewish organization
2. Nizer organization
3. Waters of Megiddo
4. Never__ JDL motto
5. *Chutzpa* (English)
6. Jonas Salk's organization
7. Prophet's offering
8. Comedian Kaye
9. Roasted on *Pesach*
10. Stone or Bronze
11. Prayer for dew
12. ___ *tadrut*
15. *Peyes*
20. Chagall specialty
22. Chanukah receipts
23. That woman
24. Leader with Aaron
25. Profession for Greenberg
26. "The Rose" actress
27. __ *Maamin*, Wiesel work
28. Haifa to Jerusalem (dir.)
30. Cain to Adam
31. Top for Gottex
33. Adam was the first

34. King and Arkin
36. Biblical fishing device
38. Freud inventions
39. 1,200
40. Got ya!
42. Bridge to Jordan
44. Plagues
45. Exist
47. Four to a *dreidel*
48. Possess

50. Cohn, Paramount Pictures
51. Singer Bubbles
52. Breaks the ninth
53. Not with meat!
54. Noah to Japhet
55. Wallach
56. Depot (abbr.)
58. __ de Toilet
60. *Shema* ender
61. Koppel

Puzzle 8

Across

1. Makes a *fey* a *pey*
4. Haifa to Hebron (dir.)
7. Tel Aviv to Ashdod (dir.)
10. Belief: comb. form
13. Kosher mammal
14. Torah breastplate
15. Tens days long
16. Depot (abbr.)
17. *Shabbat* stew
19. Philistine or Canaanite
20. Copeland on track
21. Catcher Moe
22. That one
23. Lot's wife
24. Nazi super race
26. *Teruah*
27. *Gehenna*
28. Does biblically
29. Blessed
30. Jacob Frank: __ messiah
31. Profession for Nizer
32. Pagan sun god
33. Adam was the first
34. Poetess of wit

39. Laughing sound
40. Negev climate
41. Rim
43. Demon
46. Singer or Asch
47. Zeta __ Tau, fraternity
48. Seth's dad
49. Teva offering
50. Biblical outcast
51. *Bris* must
52. Secured the *Afikoman*
53. Two included
54. *Lamed* (English)
55. Named in a *Mishaberach*
56. Prince of angels
59. 102
60. __ *Maamin*, Wiesel work
61. __ of the Covenant
62. Jerusalem to Tiberias (dir.)
63. *Yarmulke*
64. Egyptian snake
65. Platters by Manilow
66. __ *Rungs*, Buber

Down

1. 700
2. Sound of awe
3. Ark animals (3 wds)
4. Violinist Isaac
5. Imitated Neil Diamond
6. Hester Street time zone
7. El-Al specialty
8. Broke the first
   commandment

9. *K'Tonton*
10. Alias Jacob
11. Sukkahs
12. Torah cloth
18. Mom to Naphtali
22. Rona Barrett's beat
23. Seder plate item
24. Anti-Semitism
    fighters

25. Via Maris, *Sea* __
26. Japheth's dad
29. Owns biblically
30. *Kibbutz,* often
32. "High *tref* "
33. Messiah mount?
35. Dorothy Parker gift
36. "__ of Settlement"
37. Symbol of creation
38. Circumcision
42. Herman Barrron's score
43. Hebrew letter

44. Haman's fifth
45. Bride's gift to groom
46. Writer Roth
47. House (Hebrew comb. word)
49. Hebrew letters
50. *Peyes*
53. Noah's messenger
55. Travel club
56. Apple computer
57. Tel Aviv to Bet She'an (dir.)
58. Bernstein to friends

1	2	3		4	5	6		7	8	9		10	11	12
13				14				15				16		
17			18					19				20		
		21					22				23			
24	25					26					27			
28					29					30				
31				32				33						
	34		35				36				37	38		
		39				40					41		42	
43	44	45				46				47				
48					49					50				
51				52				53						
54				55				56					57	58
59				60				61				62		
63				64				65				66		

Puzzle 9

Across

1. Campaign organization
4. *Potch* (English)
7. Julius Rosenberg
10. 1,200
13. Mt. Hermon activity
14. Judah Ha-Levi specialty
15. Stooges
16. Travel club
17. Baseball player "Flip"
19. *Shiva* mood
20. King David__, Jerusalem
21. Holes
22. Calligrapher's tool
23. Dressed
24. Torah decorations
26. Bar Kochba
27. Mission for Sabin
28. Sigh
29. Hummus holder
30. *Bonanza* dad
31. Biblical measure
32. *Zaftig* (English)
33. Torah breastplate
34. Haifa sea

39. Whichever
40. Pleat
41. Admirer
43. *Tzedakah*
46. Saks or Macy's event
47. Max Baer's weapon
48. Covet
49. Comedian Dana
50. 18th king of Israel
51. Roasted on Pesach
52. Chest for tablets
53. Jolson specialty
54. Golden __ of Spain
55. Biblical herb
56. Concentration camp
59. Prayer for dew
60. Goodman or Siegal
61. Dike
62. Columnist Landers
63. Rebecca to Laban
64. Taxmen
65. *Sin* (English)
66. As born

Down

1. Israel's ally
2. Alphabet run
3. Arkia vehicle
4. Caesar and Parks
5. Fruit drinks
6. Commandments
7. Canaanite killed by a tentpin
8. Brubeck's instrument

9. Jew (Yiddish)
10. Author Norman
11. Israel at times
12. *Havdalah*
18. Chanukah need
22. *Columbo* star
23. Elected
24. *Feh* (English)
25. Twelve wells site

26. *Afikoman* action
29. Mercy
30. Polaroid's Edward
32. Manischewitz offering
33. *Agadah* (English)
35. Arrows
36. Close the Torah
37. Dessert matzoh
38. Resnik's organization
42. Last degree
43. *Shvitzes* (English)
44. Tenth minor prophet
45. *Seraphim* (English)
46. Shofar blasts
47. Like the Second Temple
49. Joyce Brothers alias
50. Ginsberg specialties
53. Political party
55. Shawn Green stat.
56. Alphabet run
57. Be'er Sheva to Jerusalem (dir.)
58. *Shema* ender

Puzzle 10

Across

1. Red Buttons act
4. Arkia posting
7. Lion's foot
10. *Kippah*
13. Mt. Hermon feature
14. Leather punch
15. Enjoyed the seder
16. Got ya!
17. First book
19. Lox starters
20. Damage
21. Beasts of burden
22. Container
23. Name on towel
24. Director DeMille
26. Called biblically
27. Victim of Zimri
28. Levaye notice
29. Jerusalem entry
30. Buckwheat groats
31. Jacob to Zebulun
32. Paddles
33. 104
34. Monty Hall show

39. *Shikker*'s choice
40. Gershwin and Levin
41. Prophesize
43. Step for Arthur Murray
46. Tribe
47. Political party
48. Sabin vaccine
49. Allen and Blanc
50. *Mitzvot*, or Good ___
51. Not on Shabbat
52. Switch positons
53. _ *No Evil*, Sharansky work
54. Belief: comb. form
55. Hester Street time zone
56. Talmud (2 wds)
59. Travel club
60. Her
61. Soak
62. Wallach
63. Biblical measure
64. Ever to Lazarus
65. Last degree
66. Israeli tax

Down

1. Job for Getz or Sedaka
2. Canasta card
3. The Holocaust
4. Equipment for Modigliani
5. Jacob to Esau
6. Capp or Jolson
7. *Adloyadah*
8. Yom Kippur must
9. *K'Tonton*

10. Ships of the Sinai
11. Benjamin's boy
12. Weekly *sidra*
18. Exodus
22. Jewish vaudeville mountains
23. Temple offering
24. Kosher fish
25. Israeli mountain
26. Actress Theda

29. Maccabiah event
30. Sacrifices often
32. Principles signing city
33. Actor James
35. Seder locale
36. Byzantine and Messianic
37. Potok character
38. Imitate Joshua
42. Eat (Yiddish)
43. Mount of Isaac's binding
44. Haman's son

45. Hitler
46. Position for Art Shamsky
47. Crest
49. General Dayan
50. *Yahrzeit* remembrance
53. Have *shpilkes* (English)
55. Tel Aviv to Jerusalem (dir.)
56. Possess
57. ___ *carte*
58. Seinfeld specialty

Puzzle 11

Across

1. Her
4. Barn
10. Joseph's dream
14. *Barney Miller*'s __ Linden
15. Alias Jacob
16. *The __*, Midler's movie
17. Mother (Hebrew)
18. Maimonides
19. Matured
20. *Mikveh*
22. *Daled* (English)
23. Pointer (Hebrew)
24. Noah before sons
26. Arkia equipment
29. Literary initials
30. Israeli city with 1 down
31. White Sox Abrams
33. Cactus
36. Sharansky
37. Cable network
38. Observe
39. Made *aliyah*
40. Commandment word
41. Vase
42. Hammerin' Hank's specialty
43. One Supreme _
44. *Shmatah* (English)
45. Son of Seth
46. Three: comb. form
47. DJ, __ the "K"
49. Like De Rothschilds
53. Eve's origin
54. Appendage
55. *Teva* offering
56. Shemini Atzeret hope
58. Li'l Abner creator
61. King David__, Jerusalem
62. Minor Prophet
63. Live on the Golan
64. Never
65. Solomon's secret
66. Last king of Israel
67. Larry Sherry stat.

Down

1. Israeli city with 30 across
2. Terrorist group
3. First Israeli ambassador to the United States
4. Title for Jacob Epstein
5. Hebrew letters
6. Packing an Uzi
7. Moses in the bullrushes
8. Meadow
9. Tu B'Shevat need
10. Pandean pipe
11. Author Richler
12. Gaza to Eilat (dir.)
13. NIS word
21. Like Esau
23. Tale
25. Business degree
26. Actor Falk
27. Seder manner
28. Oral vaccine inventor
30. Hubs for *Tsahal*
32. Samson's hair

3. Waters of Marah
4. Abraham once
5. First Israeli Prime Minister
6. *Star Trek* star
9. Columnist Barrett
0. Worn under *Chuppahs*
2. ___ Alpert, bandleader
3. Top for Gottex
6. Tisha B'av remembrance
8. Vidal product

49. Heavenly rage
50. Yours, biblically
51. Commandment word
52. Butt-in-sky, Yiddish
54. Imitates Rod Steiger
56. Isaac stand in
57. "Friend," to Wiesel
58. Mourning sign of old
59. Rabbi ___ Baeck
60. Not on *Pesach*

Puzzle 12

Across

1. Make the Challah
5. Pagan deities
10. Lee J. Cobb
13. Byzantine and Messianic
14. Golfer Amy
16. Travel club
17. Lighten
18. ___ herbs
19. *Shikker*'s choice
20. Solomon's find
21. Dreidel letter
22. Seen on gravestone
24. Torah commentator
26. Vigoda
29. To and ___
30. Singer Merman
31. Uriel's headgear
33. King of Israel
36. King and Arkin
38. Kinneret shape
40. Recede
41. Northern Israeli valley
45. Zionist Rose
47. __ *Maamin*, Wiesel book
48. Breaks the ninth
50. Jamie __ Curtis
51. Sat *shiva*
53. Moses' horns
55. Four (Hebrew)
59. *Shissel* (English)
61. Air organization
62. Broke the eighth
63. Ram's horn
66. Herman Barron need
68. *Bubkes* (English)
69. ___ *Crowd*, Birmingham
70. Israeli newspaper
73. Issachar city
74. Tay-Sachs carrier
75. The Roman ___
76. Tu B'Shevat planting
77. Number ending
78. Nisan feast
79. Job's trouble

Down

1. B.C.E. word
2. Noah's landing pad
3. Seder segment
4. Haifa to Nazareth (dir.)
5. Moses in the bullrushes
6. Up to Israel
7. Imitate Tony Randall
8. True man of Sodom
9. Stair
10. Bow and arrow holiday
11. Jonathan Pollard's residence
12. Staff
15. Non-kosher
21. Pharisees teacher
23. Gad to Simeon
25. *Shema* starter
27. *Feh*
28. King of Israel
32. Sabin vaccine
34. Shawn Green stat
35. Son of (Sephardic)
37. Edomite mountain
39. *Bivakasha* (English)

41. "___bone of an ass," Samson's weapon
42. Gaza to Jerusalem (dir.)
43. Wife to Moses
44. Eden wear?
46. Saucy
49. Literary initials
52. Hebrew letter
54. Mort Sahl's genre
56. Actress Franklin
57. Non-Hebrew tribes
58. *Tsahal* cap
60. Item on Schindler's list
63. Ache
64. Emulate Wiesenthal
65. Source for Shofars
67. Eer to Ha-Levi
71. Monkey
72. Got away
73. Likely

Puzzle 13

Across

1. ___Yar
5. Mama __ Elliott
9. Eleventh Judah King
13. Sigh
14. Anne Frank's dad
15. Political party
17. Resnik's organization
18. Singer
20. Make *challah*
22. Actor Cobb
23. *Bris* participant
24. Eilat reef
27. *Bimahs*
30. Sacrifice residue
33. Confident
34. Gelilah act
35. Sid Caesar's __ *of Shows*
37. Wealthy ancient city
39. Buckwheat groats
43. Haman's son
45. Dinah's attacker

47. Step
48. Sharansky to friends
50. Employ
51. Emulated Deborah
53. Crest
55. Not: comb. form
56. Issure Danielovitch-___, Kirk Douglas
59. Shimon
61. ___ *carte*
62. Third king of Judah
64. Use for *tzedakah*
68. Jacob's progeny
73. Victim of Zimri
74. Hammedatha's son
75. You, biblically
76. Circumcision
77. Sarah to Abraham
78. Transaction
79. Appear

Down

1. De Rothschild's organization
2. *Candid Camera's* Funt
3. Hub for *Tsahal*
4. Father of twins
5. Prisoner
6. Enjoyed manna
7. Comedian Jerry
8. Shoe base
9. *Shikker*'s choice
10. Secured the *afikoman*
11. Gulf of __

12. Paramount Pictures founder
16. Eight for Chanukah
19. Knesset position
21. Dreidel
25. Book read on Shavuot
26. Nazi super race
28. Similar
29. Ulpan function
30. Egyptian snakes
31. Salk's vaccine
32. Dance

36. Sounds at the Western wall?
38. Lauder
40. *Tefillin* letter
41. Mordechai
42. So be it
44. *Star __*, Shatner's voyage
46. *Shema* starter
49. Haman's third son
52. Singer Cannon
54. Nimoy casually
56. Maccabiah race

57. Bath-Sheba's dad
58. Zilpah to Asher
60. Ezekiel and Isaiah
63. Observes shiva
65. *Dawn* author
66. Sukkah decoration
67. Ham's brother
69. *Ess* (English)
70. *Echad* (English)
71. Wiggling *treif* fish
72. Prophesize

1	2	3	4		5	6	7	8		9	10	11	12	
13					14					15				16
17					18			19						
20			21			22					23			
		24		25	26			27	28	29				
30	31	32		33				34						
35			36		37		38		39		40	41	42	
43			44				45	46						
47					48	49				50				
		51		52		53			54		55			
56	57	58				59				60				
61				62	63				64		65	66	67	
68			69	70			71	72		73				
74					75				76					
	77				78				79					

Puzzle 14

Across

1. *Gabbai* catch
5. Musician Getz
9. *Mr. __*, Lorre film
13. *Tzedakah*
14. Wanderer
15. Israelite city
16. Rebecca's brother
17. Negev climate
18. Kinneret
19. Pagan deity
20. Emulated Spitz
21. Hammerin' Hank's specialty
22. Plotting Persian guard
24. Second Temple enhancer
26. *Vav* (English)
27. Nizer and Kunstler
31. Actor Curtis
34. Section
36. *My Life*, Meir story
37. Joseph's dream
38. Arthur Murray milieu
39. Writer Howard
40. *Mems* (English)
41. *Greps* (English)
42. *Chuppah* holders
43. Cantor Rosenblatt
45. Israelite city
46. Harry Houdini alias
48. Plays for Jan Peerce
52. Kabbalistic book
55. Dreidels
57. Raphael's aura
58. Eer to Ha-Levi
59. Kedem drinkers?
60. President of Travelers
61. Larry Sherry's club
62. Mechanical designer (abbr.)
63. Enjoyed the *Seder*
64. Murray and Shamsky
65. Job's trouble
66. Utopia

Down

1. Oasis offering
2. Bitter work
3. *Rosemary's Baby* author
4. *Treif* hangout
5. Bandleader
6. Books of Moses
7. Philistine king
8. Cain's refuge
9. Rodgers and Hammerstein specialty
10. World (Hebrew)
11. Winnings
12. Grain measure
13. Like *shiva* clothes
20. Her
21. Writer Irving
23. Prophesize
25. Maccabiah game
28. Israeli mountain
29. Make *aliyah*
30. *Shikkers*
31. Comedian Bishop

32. Stones for David
33. *Mishmash* (English)
34. Israel at times
35. Corporation
38. Jewish restaurant
39. *Tefillin* location
41. Purim drink
42. Jacob to Dinah
44. Plague
45. David O. Selznick

47. Helen Reddy specialty
49. *Hagba'ah*
50. Woody
51. Auction word
52. __ Beta Tau, fraternity
53. Angel of Death path
54. Negev condition
56. Haifa or Ashdod
59. Soak
60. *K'Tonton*

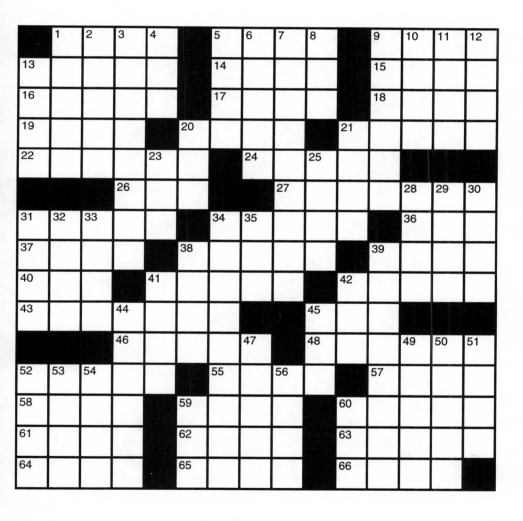

Puzzle 15

Across

1. Multi-colored coat
5. Eighth day event
9. Deli fare listing
13. Torah decorations
14. Calligraphy needs
15. Angel of Death path
16. Singer Cantor
17. Diary writer Frank
18. 1,003
19. Magic Carpet base
20. Goliath
21. Elim offerings
22. Lulav part
24. Oral vaccine inventor
27. *Zetz* (English)
29. David's triumphs
33. Cosmetic mogul
36. *Eretz* (English)
38. __ mode
39. Sigh
40. Roberta Peters' specialties
41. Emulate Spitz
42. Leah's sons
43. King David's specialty
44. Montefiore
45. Read at the unveiling
47. Pomegranate plenty
49. Leah to Rachel
51. Moe or Larry
55. Hammedatha's son
58. *Mems* (English)
60. Naomi at times?
61. Sinai climate
62. *Tekiah*
64. Solomon
65. Kinneret
66. Shaw and Shamsky
67. *Tref* hangouts
68. Judah Ha-Levi specialty
69. Dead and Red
70. Jerualem to Tel Aviv (dir.)

Down

1. Singer Helen
2. Simeon to Gad
3. *Blinis*
4. Haifa to Degania (dir.)
5. ___ Brak
6. Given under *Chupahs*
7. Son of (Sephardic)
8. Ashdod to Be'ersheba (dir.)
9. Jewish magazine
10. __ Eye
11. Singer Diamond
12. *Exodus* author
13. Moses' horn
20. Artist Shahn
21. Including
23. Break the ninth
25. Baseball player Cal
26. Greenberg tools
28. Biblical weights
30. Ten commandments
31. *Dawn* author
32. Levinson and Goldwyn
33. *Seder* manner

34. Gabbai catch
35. Cab
37. Need chicken soup
40. Egyptian snakes
41. Hedonist
43. Ache
44. Shamsky was one
46. Hebrew letters
48. *Sin* (English)
50. Butt-in-sky (Yiddish)

52. Desert sweetspot
53. *Shalom!*
54. *Hamantaschen*
55. Michael's aura
56. Israeli silver medalist
57. Wallace of *60 Minutes*
59. *Mishmash* (English)
62. Torah breastplate
63. Solomon's find
64. Jerusalem to Ashkelon (dir.)

Puzzle 16

Across

1. Pomegranate plenty
5. Maccabiah game
9. __ shekel, Temple dues
13. Dead Sea cosmetics
14. World (Hebrew)
15. Talmud, __ Law
16. Levite domain
17. Hebrew letters
18. Etrog's cousin
19. Matzoh maker's need
20. Borscht base
21. Gave *tzedakah*
22. Tribal member
24. Kol__
26. Young louse
27. Etrogs
31. Plague
34. Orthodox minyan
36. Makes a *fey* a *pey*
37. Imitates Rickles
38. Montefiore
39. Zeta __ Tau, fraternity
40. Employ
41. Eating utensils
42. Solomonic
43. Acted the *Yenta*
45. Poodle
46. Desert cool spots
48. *Samech* or *lamed*
52. 1996 United States Olympic Gold medalist, gymnastics
55. Eighteen (Hebrew)
57. Raphael's aura
58. Ishmael progeny
59. Seventh king
60. *Bris* stars
61. Diamond or Simon
62. Transaction
63. Book of __
64. Actor Hackman
65. *Tel* (English)
66. Move swiftly

Down

1. Mourning week
2. Adam's apple
3. Ma'ariv times
4. __*Kapital*, Marx work
5. Zionist Halprin
6. Non-Hebrew tribe
7. Song of Songs
8. *Mems* (English)
9. More sacred
10. Sinai climate
11. Jacob after the angel
12. Departed
13. Gad's boy
20. Genesis starter
21. Bezalel specialty
23. It is, to Ha-Levi
25. Expires
28. Dorothy Parker specialties
29. *Tekiah* or *Teruah*
30. Magen David
31. Observant
32. Make *aliyah*
33. Ruth's son
34. Purim hero

35. Imitate the four sons
38. Berg and a Stooge
39. Persian guard
41. Blue and White banner
42. *Shiva* mood
44. *Lamedvav* to *chai*
45. 551
47. Biblical word
49. Mountain
50. Choose
51. __ Hashanah
52. Emulated Barry Manilow
53. Life or Knowledge
54. Forty day forecast
56. Cain's victim
59. Mourning sign of old
60. *Divan*

Puzzle 17

Across

1. *Noodge* (English)
4. Hebrew letter
7. *Pay* without the dot
10. Prepare for Seder
13. Tay Sachs carrier
14. In front of
15. ___ mode
16. Ithamar high priest
17. Fourth commandment
19. "Sea" to Wiesel
20. Portion (abbr.)
21. *Shikker* stops
22. Jacob's sore spot
23. Own
24. Tribes
26. Elliott Gould film
27. Tenth part of an ephah
28. Mt. Hermon climate
29. Maccabiah race
30. Rainbows
31. Finance degree
32. Lear to his friends
33. Heschel to friends
34. Haman's hat (2 words)
39. Greenberg stat.
40. *Tzedakah* purpose
41. Reason for *shiva*
43. Like *shiva* clothes
46. Closure
47. Jaw ___ of an ass, Samson's weapon
48. Listen
49. *Simcha* (English)
50. Dreidel letter
51. Tu B'Shevat plantings
52. Copeland on track
53. ___Yar
54. *Bet* (English)
55. Tri *chai*
56. Pre-Israelites
59. "I ___ Thou", Martin Buber
60. Gaza to Jerusalem (dir.)
61. *Shikker*'s choice
62. Byzantine or Messianic
63. Dreidel letter
64. Classifieds
65. Torah breastplate
66. Leah's sons

Down

1. Freud inventions
2. Tay Sachs carrier
3. Mysticism
4. Seder water
5. Shaw and Shamsky
6. Yiddish disdain
7. Tisha B'av condition
8. Hebrew letter
9. Babi ___ , Ukraine
10. Tahina
11. Joseph's brothers
12. Greenberg's team
18. Klezmatics
22. Western Wall tunnel
23. Hammerin' Hank's specialty
24. Gideon's best men
25. Attic

26. Chagall
29. *Macher* (English)
30. Ruth's son
32. *Nebbish* (English)
33. Issachar city
35. Moses camoflage
36. Chant Torah
37. Esau's progeny
38. *Seder* action
42. Wiggling *treif* fish
43. Biblical well site

44. Cosmetic lady
45. Chicken soup
46. Hebrews in Egypt
47. Netenyahu nickname
49. Crush
50. Maccabian or Olympic
53. Abzug
55. Meadow
56. Used his *tuches*
57. Son of Gad
58. Getz instrument

Puzzle 18

Across

1. *Schnoorer* (English)
4. *Barney Miller's* __ Linden
7. Yiddish disdain
10. Torah breastplate
13. Wallach
14. Son of Gad
15. B'nai B'rith youth organization
16. Cable network
17. Likely
18. *Schmooz* (English)
19. Supply with Uzis
20. Amen
21. Ben Yehuda, Jerusalem
23. Name
25. Modigliani
27. *Treif* crawler
29. Smidgen
31. Shofar blast
32. Nebo or Sinai
34. Midler
36. __ *mode*
38. Shofar note
40. __ *of Settlement*
44. Wailing Wall today
46. Canadian writer
48. Seder manner
49. Torah chanter
51. *Maude* star
52. Ezra's swift scribe
54. Stooge Larry
56. Choose
59. Sabin's milieu
61. Noah's messengers
64. *Fleishidic* and *milkedic*
66. Peace __, political organization
68. Jazzman Getz
69. Received
70. Jacob to Naphtali
72. Miller or Fielder
74. Literary initials
75. Afula to Degania (dir.)
76. Geller
77. Cheer
78. Tu B' Shevat planting
79. Tel-Aviv to Hebron (dir.)
80. Sopher need
81. Julius Rosenberg?
82. Be'ersheba to Jerusalem (dir.)

Down

1. Moses' horns?
2. Hebrew school
3. Uris novel (2 words)
4. *Fey* with a dot
5. Israeli silver medalist
6. Political party
7. Air organization
8. Prophet
9. __ Gader, hot springs
10. Actress Bara
11. Joab's victim
12. Hedonist haven
22. Bear false witness
24. ___Yar

26. Hebrew letter
28. Tardy
30. Nazarite growth
33. Olympian Strug
35. *Gonif* (English)
36. Tens days long
37. Meadow
39. Jolson's postion
41. *Chico and the Man* star
42. Jamie __ Curtis
43. Larry Sherry stat.
45. Ulpan function
47. Baby holder

50. *Candid Camera's* Funt
53. Make aliyah (2 words)
55. Israeli coin
56. *Tsitsit* site
57. Signs for Judah
58. Lauder
60. *Treif* males
62. Yael __, author
63. Eden denizen
65. Ache
67. Put on *tefillin*
71. Target for Mark Roth
73. Thou possessive

Puzzle 19

Across

1. Identical
5. Koufax specialty
10. Hebrew letter
13. *Schmutz* (English)
15. Mount of tablets
16. Aaron's resting place
17. Vidal product
18. Leap year month
20. Einstein action
21. Pointer (Hebrew)
23. Galilee and Dead
24. *Lulav frond*
26. Catcher Moe
29. Levite domain
32. *Scum* author
34. __ *Crowd*, Birmingham novel
36. Not on *Shabbat*
37. Business degree
38. Rosenblatt specialty
40. Jerusalem to Tiberias (dir.)
41. Classifieds
44. Got ya!

46. United States Mossad?
47. Zilpah's boy
48. *Feh*
49. *Eretz* (English)
51. Gaza to Jerusalem (dir.)
53. *Erevs* (English)
55. Radioman Allen
56. Exodus egress
60. Miriam at times
62. Fog
64. Barter
65. *Negev* condition
67. Dried grass
69. *Tefillin*
70. Israeli city
74. Dead Sea cosmetics
76. Ribicoff
77. "Great" king of Judea
78. Greenberg specialty
79. Jew (Yiddish)
80. Graven__
81. *Minyans*

Down

1. Tefillin features
2. Haman's ninth
3. Almonds (Yiddish)
4. *Sin* (English)
5. Hebrew letter
6. Secured the *afikoman*
7. Tay-Sachs carrier
8. Paddles
9. Solomon
10. Paul Newman film (2 words)

11. Long period
12. Three: comb. form
14. *Fey* with a dot
19. Samson's strength
22. Fortas or Geiger
25. Mayer company
27. Act the *gonif*
28. Eilat waters
30. Author Ferber
31. Pomegranate plenty
33. Mountain

35. Singer Peters
39. Kedem or Schapiro offering
41. Cain's victim
42. Pianist Brubeck
43. Hebrew profession
45. Issachar city
50. 551
52. Koch and Teller
54. Isaiah or Samuel
57. Tahina

58. Joseph's brothers
59. *Bimahs*
61. Torah commentator
63. Oasis offering
66. Those people
68. Slang affirmation
70. Haifa
71. __ de Toilet
72. Larry Sherry stat.
73. Marsh
75. Tiberias springs

1	2	3	4		5	6	7	8	9		10	11	12
13				14	15						16		
17					18					19			
20				21	22			23					
24			25		26		27	28		29		30	31
32				33			34		35		36		
		37				38			39		40		
41	42	43		44		45		46				47	
48				49		50		51		52			
53			54		55				56		57	58	59
60				61		62		63			64		
		65			66			67		68		69	
70	71					72	73			74	75		
76				77						78			
79				80						81			

Puzzle 20

Across

1. King and Arkin
4. Lillian Florence Hellman
7. Actor Cobb
10. Noah's boy
13. Age
14. Exist
15. Literary initials
16. Long before
17. *Havdalah* candle
19. Greenberg or Rosen
21. Negev climate
22. Subway fare
24. Move swiftly
25. Ancient dynasty
27. *Bubkes* (English)
28. Asher's boy
29. Puppeteer
31. Also
32. Supply with Uzis
35. First Jewish Miss America
36. Rachel to Issachar
40. *Bris* star
42. Giant Dead Sea tribe
44. Lion's lairs
45. Duke of Edom
47. Sharansky to friends
49. Be'er sheva to Hebron (dir.)
50. Hadassah employees
51. Alexander the __
53. Torah crown (Hebrew)
56. Ever to Bialik
57. *Schmutz*
61. Imitates
62. Bitter water station
64. Son of Samuel
65. *Star Trek* star
67. Touro Synagogue site
69. Aaron's resting place
70. Chanukah miracle
71. Solomon's find
72. Prophesize
73. Classifieds
74. Sinai climate
75. Haifa to Jerusalem (dir.)
76. Amen

Down

1. Four (Hebrew)
2. *Mr. Moto* star
3. Step
4. *Yeled* (English)
5. *Shpilkes* (English)
6. Gomorrah sin
7. Blood __
8. Former Israeli ambassador
9. Eat (Yiddish)
10. Villain in Shushan
11. 100th of an NIS
12. *Av* or *Tammuz*
18. Pagan deity
20. Baron __ de Rothschild
23. United States Secretary of State under Nixon
26. Winger to friends
28. Usurious instrument
30. Shavuot (English)
31. *Ta'am* (English)

32. Nizer organization
33. *Shofar* source
34. Business degree
37. Minyan men
38. King David__, Jerusalem
39. Haifa to Tiberias (dir.)
41. Simeon
43. Secret Jews
46. Al Rosen stat.
48. Enjoy *latkes*
52. Snare

53. Buckwheat groats
54. High priest vestment
55. Seder water
56. Premature
58. Made *aliyah*
59. Shofar blast
60. Acted the bigot
62. Golda
63. Name on towel
66. Cain's refuge
68. K'Tonton

1	2	3		4	5	6		7	8	9		10	11	12
13				14				15				16		
17			18					19			20			
21					22		23				24			
25				26		27				28				
			29		30				31					
32	33	34		35					36			37	38	39
40			41		42			43			44			
45				46			47			48		49		
			50				51				52			
53	54	55				56				57		58	59	60
61					62			63			64			
65				66				67		68				
69				70				71				72		
73				74				75				76		

Puzzle 21

Across

1. *Fay* (English)
4. Her
7. *Schnoor* (English)
10. *Yarmulke*
13. 52
14. Prepare for Seder
15. Bo Belinsky stat.
16. Freud invention
17. Bernstein to friends
18. Sid Gordon's stat
19. __ Aviv
20. Torah
21. Gershwin and Morris
23. Gang for Bugsy Siegal
25. Perlman's piece
27. Touro
30. Symbols of Judah
31. Tribe
32. Sinai ship?
34. Prepared *latkes*
36. Stooges
37. *Bet* (English)
40. Ribicoff and Vigoda
41. Played canasta
42. Tu B'Shevat plantings
43. El-Al milieu
44. Bagel's cousin
45. Dung and Jaffa
46. Choose
47. Moses' miracle
48. Israeli coin
51. Sodomites
55. Seder segment
57. Greenberg stat.
58. Teva offering
59. B'nai B'rith organization (abbr.)
60. Dreidel
62. Jerusalem to Tiberias (dir.)
64. Seth's mom
65. Shalom
66. Mother (Hebrew)
67. Named in a *mishaberach*
68. __ Ilan street, Jerusalem
69. Ribicoff
70. Daniel's test site
71. Radioman Allen
72. Expressions of ease

Down

1. Island entry
2. Like Moses' bush
3. Haym Salomon
4. Haifa to Hebron (dir.)
5. Israeli mountain
6. Lulav companion
7. Genesis starter
8. Eve (Hebrew)
9. Lake Kinneret?
10. American shalom
11. *Never* __, Kahane book
12. Shtetls
22. Comic Soupy
24. Louis "Lepke" ___, crime figure
26. Chanukah miracle
28. Jacob's boy
29. Premature

33. Encountered
34. Air organization
35. Sid Gordon's stat.
36. Ulpan function
37. David's sweetie
38. __ out a living
39. *Sin* (English)
41. Reason for *shiva*
42. Desert sweet spot
44. Sounded the shofar
45. Uzi

46. In front of
47. Actress Franklin
48. Eilat gulf
49. *Chad __*, song
50. JPSA founder, Cyrus
52. Israeli land measure
53. *Shanah ___* (Hebrew)
54. Samuel and Amos
56. Moe Berg's plate
61. *Shissel* (English)
63. *Lamed* (English)

1	2	3		4	5	6		7	8	9		10	11	12
13				14				15				16		
17				18				19				20		
21			22		23		24		25		26			
27				28				29		30				
		31					32		33					
34	35					36						37	38	39
40					41						42			
43				44					45					
			46						47					
48	49	50				51		52					53	54
55					56		57				58			
59				60		61		62		63		64		
65				66				67				68		
69				70				71				72		

Puzzle 22

Across

1. Moses' last mount
5. Poet Lazarus
9. *Aggadah*
13. Like Adam's apple
14. Author Dayan
15. Tishri to Elul
16. *Bonanza* dad
17. Prophet of synagogues
18. Barrett
19. Minor Prophet
20. Employ
21. Klezmer groups
22. Chanukah sight
24. Jacob's father-in-law
27. Eleventh king of Judah
29. Observes *Shabbat*
33. Use a *mikveh*
36. Lauder
38. Lox starters
39. Former Israeli ambassador
40. Rothstein nickname
41. Spar
42. *Lamed* (English)
43. Use for *tzedakah*
44. Roasted on *Pesach*
45. Actor Peter
47. Seder salt water
49. Jerusalem gates
51. Hatikvah
55. *Love Story* writer
58. *Streimel*
60. Jan Peerce specialty
61. Israeli city
62. "__ Trek," Nimoy's show
64. Purim faces
65. Speechless
66. *Merkavah*
67. Swindle
68. Eer to Ha-Levi
69. Youngman hope
70. Tribe

Down

1. Ruth's mother-in-law
2. Citron
3. Artist and illustrator
4. *Echad* (English)
5. Soul windows
6. __ *Tov* (Good Luck)
7. "Sea" to Wiesel
8. __ carte
9. Antiochus
10. Long time
11. *Eretz* (English)
12. Byzantine and Messianic
13. Security experts
20. Israel's ally
21. Shamsky goal
23. "__ Accident," by Wiesel
25. Baskin or Raskin
26. Existed
28. Haman's wife
30. Esther's kingdom?
31. *Schnozz* (English)
32. Divorce papers
33. *Bets* (English)
34. Skillful

35. Goliath
37. Tisha B'av mood
40. Baseball spy?
41. Comedian
43. Sedaka or Simon
44. Prohibit
46. Moses or Deborah
48. Enjoy *cholent*
50. *Bevakasha* (English)
52. First minor prophet

53. Sculptor Benno
54. Greatest
55. Identical
56. *Shabbat* border
57. Golden or Herod
59. Torah homes
62. Chazzer house
63. Zeta Beta ___, fraternity
64. 1,200

Puzzle 23

Across

1. Kosher must
4. Modern chariot
7. Tiberias to Tel Aviv (dir.)
10. Olympian Friedman
13. Nizer organization
14. Geller
15. Sabin's organization
16. Anger
17. Negev and Sinai
19. Torah breastplate
20. On the __
21. Glorify
22. Fromm or Segal
24. Gad to Simeon
25. Commandment no no
27. *Noodge* (English)
28. Comedienne Rivers
29. Mother (Hebrew)
32. Masada event
34. Sacrifices often
35. The strip
37. Lillian Florence Hellman monogram
38. Scream

39. *Bench* (3 words)
45. *Zetz* (English)
46. Ever to Nelly Sachs
47. Danny DeVito's wife
48. Moabite king
51. Joseph's coat feature
53. Einstein activity
54. Magic Carpet base
55. __ de Toilet
56. Parted sea
58. Round for Spitz
59. Cohen's hands
61. Simeon
65. *Shikker*'s choice
66. Classifieds
67. Esau's progeny
69. Arkia milieu
70. Golden girl Arthur
71. Neither's partner
72. Jacob's boy
73. Rachel and Leah
74. Moe Berg stat.
75. Dike
76. Amen

Down

1. Lighten
2. Shofar source
3. Resnik's organization
4. Tony or Jamie Lee
5. Baseball's Shamsky
6. Make *aliyah*
7. Mort Sahl's genre
8. *Potch* (English)
9. Use a *mikveh*

10. Mount near Afula
11. Noah's landing pad
12. Etrog cousins
18. *Lamed* (English)
23. Oscar Schindler
26. Scuba diving city
28. Rickles or Seinfeld
29. Roasted on Pesach
30. Damage

31. B'nai B'rith youth organization
33. *Fay* (English)
34. Eilat stone
36. Hid Jericho spoils
38. Gabbai catch
40. Prior NYC mayor
41. Wiggling *treif* fish
42. Got ya!
43. Emulated Moses
44. *Shiva* mood
48. Balak's prophet

49. Haman's fifth
50. Biblical outcasts
51. Emcee Sid
52. Wise's movement
55. Methusaleh
57. Faint
59. Moses in the bullrushes
60. Transmit
62. Not on *Shabbat*
63. Jazzman Getz
64. Watch the flock
68. Reason for *shiva*

Puzzle 24

Across

1. The Golden __
5. Benny Goodman specialty
10. *Pisk* (Yiddish)
13. Jerusalem Post
14. Horseradish
15. *Shikker*'s choice
16. Vacant
17. Emulate Abba Eban
18. El-Al posting
19. Jamie __ Curtis
20. Succot activity
22. Herman Barron shot
24. Snare
26. Moses' horn
29. Seder water
31. Deli fare
33. Exodus egress
35. Tu B'shvat object
36. *Shmatah* (English)
37. __ *shekel*, temple dues
39. Stone or Bronze
40. Japheth's brother
43. Salk's milieu
45. Archaeological mound

46. Generation (Hebrew)
47. Ellis Isle time zone
48. Breaks the ninth commandment
50. Yiddish disdain
52. Political party
54. Nimoy casually
55. *Bihemas* (English)
59. Asher's daughter
61. Maccabiah game
63. You, biblically
64. Jewish camp
66. Enjoyed *manna*
68. Exist
69. Title for Montefiore
70. Regal
73. Political party
75. Depot (abbr.)
76. Make *aliyah*
77. Einstein specialty
78. Soak
79. Aaron's oldest son
80. Elliott Gould film

Down

1. Stieglitz equipment
2. UJA word
3. Rent
4. Mimic, David
5. Killed biblically
6. Six days long
7. Gershwin
8. *Tekiah*
9. Herod the __

10. Israeli Olympic winner (Judo)
11. Freud invention
12. Not on *Pesach*
13. Jacob's disguise
21. Columnist Van Buren
23. Divorce paper
25. Amy Alcott's score
27. Sacrifice residue

28. Fleischidic (English)
30. Amos or Nahum
32. Ben Yehuda, Jerusalem
34. Hebrew letters
38. Exodus
40. Myra, pianist
41. Jacob's progeny
42. Ark landing site (2 words)
44. Boxer Max
49. Tay-Sachs carrier
51. *Yarmulke*
53. Goldwyn to friends

56. Uses his *lulav*
57. Shofar blast
58. Hamantaschen filling
60. Abraham's bro
62. Scout
65. Dance
67. Twelve wells site
69. Tiberias to Tel Aviv (dir.)
71. Jew (Yiddish)
72. Third king of Judah
74. Girl's name

Puzzle 25

Across

1. Tens days long
4. *Tsitsit* site
7. American Mossad
10. Yom Kippur or Gulf
13. Got away
14. *Shikker*'s choice
15. Third king of Judah
16. Ithamar high priest
17. Total
18. Fabergé founder (2 words)
21. Make the bagels
23. Messiah mount?
24. Dead and Red
25. *Shvitz* (English)
27. Tay-Sachs carrier
28. Evil eye
29. ___Yar
31. *Tuches* (English)
33. Tu B'Shevat need
36. Blue and White banner
38. David's weapons
42. Buddy Rich specialty
44. Choose

46. Imitates Rickles
47. Leonard and Kaplan
49. Those people
51. Break the ninth
52. Head (Hebrew)
54. Long time
56. Fourth letter of Alephbet
59. Sighs
61. *Mikvehs*
65. Freud inventions
66. Tref crawler
68. Bialik specialty
69. Moses Ben Nachman
72. Geller
73. Noodge
74. ___ *carte*
75. Sopher need
76. Age
77. Zilpah and Rachel
78. Last degree
79. 1,501
80. Nelly Sachs specialty

Down

1. Ishmael progeny
2. Ruth or Naomi
3. Singer Cantor
4. Owns
5. King of Israel
6. Yad Vashem
7. Emcee Sid
8. Ellis
9. Ribicoff
10. Artist Max

11. Golda Meir or Meyerson
12. Sasoon's product
19. Vase
20. Money lender
22. Salk's milieu
26. Hebrew letter
28. *Kippa*
30. Say Kiddush
32. Lauder
33. Recede

34. Scholar Baeck
35. Stern or Baer
37. Divorce paper
39. Need chicken soup?
40. Al Rosen stat.
41. Haifa to Hebron (dir.)
43. Plotting Persian guard
45. Amish look-alikes?
48. Actor Steiger
50. Organization for Meyer Lansky
53. Mom of seven sons

55. *Shluf* (English)
56. Strauss' jeans
57. 100th of an NIS
58. Samson's strength
60. Israeli conquest
62. Rhode Island synagogue
63. "Great" king of Judea
64. Kill biblically
66. Lot's wife
67. Imitate de Rothschild
70. Adam was the first
71. Mt. Hermon activity

1	2	3		4	5	6		7	8	9		10	11	12
13				14				15				16		
17				18			19				20			
21			22		23						24			
25				26		27				28				
			29		30			31	32					
33	34	35		36			37		38			39	40	41
42			43		44			45			46			
47				48			49			50		51		
			52			53		54			55			
56	57	58				59	60			61		62	63	64
65					66				67		68			
69				70						71		72		
73				74				75				76		
77				78				79				80		

Puzzle 26

Across

1. Singer Bubbles
6. Sid Gordon's stat.
9. Shamsky's team
13. Ezra's swift scribe
14. Travel club
15. *Shivah* sounds
17. Saul Bellow novel (2 words)
19. Johnny Kling specialty
20. Girl's name
21. Little bit
23. *Teva* offering
24. Zilpah's sons
27. *Lamed* (English)
29. *Yarmulke*
31. Amen
32. *Rosh* (English)
34. In vogue
36. Nazarite feature
38. Lauder
40. *Tuches*
42. Mrs. Rosenberg
43. Before

44. Mountain
48. El-Al equipment
50. Killed biblically
51. PLO leader
54. __ Aviv
56. Observes *shiva*
57. In front of
58. Emcee Caesar
60. Arkia milieu
62. Tried and true man
63. Resnik's organization
65. Noah to Japhet
67. American Mossad
69. Barter
71. Current Prime Minister
76. Hebrew letter
77. Paul Newman's hobby
78. Comic Soupy
79. *Minyans*
80. Wallach
81. Amalek

Down

1. Used his *tuches*
2. Sort of (ending)
3. Break the ninth
4. Second *aliyah*
5. Joe Ginsberg into home
6. Enjoy manna
7. Entebbe rescue
8. Jewish camp
9. 1,200
10. Byzantine and Roman
11. Gives 10%

12. Idolatry commandment
16. Sukkot
18. The Golden __
22. ___Yar
24. You, biblically
25. Jerualem to Tel Aviv (dir.)
26. *The __*, Wiesel book
28. Jacob's father-in-law
30. Desert homes
33. Jonah's travels?
35. Bare biblically

37. *Get Smart* guy
39. Island entry
41. Minor prophet
45. Make the bagels
46. Anne Frank's dad
47. Observe Shabbat
49. Negev climate
51. Streisand film
52. Noah's landing pad
53. Tahina
55. Plague

59. Hora
61. Vidal product
64. Magic Carpet base
66. Monty Hall specialty
68. Alephbet member
70. Cantor and Goldman
72. Three: comb. form
73. Purim drink
74. *Tsitsit* site
75. United Synagogue Youth

Puzzle 27

Across

1. Biblical judge
4. "Sea" to Chagall
7. Business degree
10. Greenberg's stat.
13. 100 *agarot*
14. ___ mode
15. Ribicoff
16. __ *Crowd*, by Birmingham
17. Joseph's son
19. Yeshiva
21. Leah to Issachar
22. Biblical garb
23. Where *Zaide* went
25. Jacob to Esau
27. Magen David
30. Nelly Sachs specialty
31. Be'er Sheva region
33. *Tzedakah* recipients
34. Gilead medicine
36. Pointer
37. Wimpel
38. Noah's rainbow
40. Dead Sea plenty
41. Murray lessons
44. Eilat stone
45. Auction word
49. Make *aliyah*
50. Biblical outcast
52. Exam for Nizer
53. *Shiva* clothes
54. Third son of Adam
55. Gimbel and Sandler
57. Butt-in-sky (Yiddish)
59. Toting an Uzi
61. Via Maris
63. *Schmutz* (English)
66. Sopher need
67. Enjoyed the Seder
68. Tay-Sachs carrier
69. Third king of Judah
70. King and Arkin
71. That one
72. Belief: comb. form
73. *Tsitsit* site

Down

1. Dor to Zippori (dir.)
2. *Chutzpah*
3. Hagar's son
4. *Ani* __, Wiesel work
5. Twelve wells site
6. Diamond center
7. Israeli newspaper
8. *Treif* strip
9. Israeli neighbor
10. *Pesach* egg
11. *Schnoor* (English)
12. Anger
18. Isaac stand-in
20. Negev and Sinai
23. Gang for Bugsy Siegel
24. Girl's name
26. Sign a *ketubah*
28. B'nai B'rith organization
29. Deli bread
32. Soul windows
33. *Bubkes* (English)
35. Meyer Lansky

37. Dreidel
39. Stooge
40. Jews of Spain
41. Damage
42. Exist
43. Tens of adults
44. Divorce paper
46. Fourth minor prophet
47. On the __
48. Freud and Sabin

50. Moses or David
51. Maimonides
54. Israel in 1948
56. Winger to friends
58. Japheth's dad
60. Greenberg's specialty
61. Ein gedi
62. Wiggling treif fish
64. Haifa to Hebron (dir.)
65. Noah's son

1	2	3		4	5	6		7	8	9		10	11	12
13				14				15				16		
17		18						19		20				
		21						22						
23	24					25	26				27		28	29
30				31	32				33					
34		35		36				37						
		38	39				40							
41	42	43				44				45	46	47	48	
49				50				51		52				
53				54				55	56					
	57		58				59	60						
61	62						63				64	65		
66			67				68			69				
70			71				72			73				

Puzzle 28

Across

1. Hebrew letter
5. Comedian Jackie
10. Actor Hackman
14. Comedian Danny
15. Graven__
16. "A Priest with __ and Thummim"
17. Cain's victim
18. Kol__
19. "__ 18," Uris novel
20. Noah's story
22. Esau
24. Long before
26. Ishmael progeny
28. First minor prophet
32. Karpas
34. Terriorists
37. Needs a *Meeshebairach*
38. Duke of Edom
40. Prayer for dew
41. Poet Lazarus
42. *Schnozes* (English)
44. Bet She'an marketplace
46. Used a shofar
48. NYC time zone
50. Broke the commandments
53. Moses' aura
54. Emulate Eban
56. Jacob to Gad
57. Sills specialty
59. Lighten
61. United Synagogue Youth
62. Tenth part of an *ephah*
65. Mountain
67. Need at Ellis Isle
70. Etrog partner
72. Diary writer
75. Byzantine and Roman
76. Moses on the mount
77. Ephraim and Manasseh
78. Scriptures
79. Media
80. Source for Seder shanks

Down

1. Alias
2. Sabin's milieu
3. Biblical punishment? (4 words)
4. Like the Second Temple
5. Hosea and Micah
6. Standing prayer
7. *Shiva* mood
8. Goliath
9. *Tzedakah* purpose
10. Marx brother
11. Son of Gad
12. *Bubkes* (English)
13. Mother (Hebrew)
21. Desert cool spots
23. Vowels
24. Got ya!
25. Eilat stone
27. Hammerin' Hank's tool
29. Great Russian Historian
30. Tu B'Shevat need
31. ___ *carte*

33. Rosenblatt specialty
35. Apple computer
36. Sigh
39. Observe Sabbath
41. Writer Ferber
43. Gaza to Be'er Sheva (dir.)
45. Never on *Shabbat*
46. Judah to Zebulun
47. Round for Spitz
49. Hebrew letter
51. Asner and Koch
52. Elie Wiesel novel
54. Prophet and judge, casually

55. Rabbi Meir
58. Prepare Seder egg
60. Noah's messengers
63. Esther's kingdom
64. The Golden __
66. Seder manner
67. Tsahal graduate
68. Anger
69. Getz instrument
71. Airport
73. Be'er Sheva to Jerusalem (dir.)
74. *Sin* (English)

1	2	3	4		5	6	7	8	9		10	11	12	13
14					15						16			
17					18						19			
		20		21				22		23				
24	25			26			27			28		29	30	31
32			33			34		35	36			37		
38				39		40				41				
		42			43		44		45					
46	47				48		49		50				51	52
53				54				55		56				
57			58				59		60			61		
		62		63	64		65			66				
67	68	69			70		71				72		73	74
75					76						77			
78					79						80			

Puzzle 29

Across

1. Isaac stand-in
4. Ruth's son
8. Bear false witness
13. Utilize
14. Slight bit
15. Like a wedding glass
16. Negative
17. Airline
18. Bet She'an builders
19. Writer Ferber
21. Graven__
23. Shimon
25. Kristalnacht casualty
26. 1,200
29. Ellis
30. Moses' horns?
31. Matriarchs
32. Airport posting
33. Use a *mikveh*
34. Israeli airline
35. Use for *tzedakah*
37. Potato pancake
39. David's dad
41. Bea Arthur role
43. Which one?
46. Kinneret
47. Sunbathes
48. Mark of __
49. *Battle* __, Uris novel
50. Messiah mount
51. Dead Sea plenty
52. *Gelt*
53. Marx
54. Sinai
57. Chimed
59. *Shikker*'s choice?
62. Abandoned married woman (Hebrew)
63. Einstein specialty
64. Container
65. Investments in Israel
66. Magic Carpet base
67. Seder shank source

Down

1. Greenberg stat.
2. Third king of Judah
3. Gangster
4. Rainbows
5. Abzug
6. Hellenistic or Biblical
7. Samson's sweetie
8. Plague
9. Empire over Israel
10. Alias
11. Orthodox *minyan*
12. *Nuns* (English)
15. Alpert's Tijuana __
20. Daled (English)
22. Palestine era
23. Soupy's ammo
24. Ellis Island time zone
25. Don Adams show (2 words)
26. *60 Minutes* anchor
27. 102
28. American Mossad
30. Haman or Amalek

31. *Noodge* (English)
33. *Bet* (English)
34. Enjoyed *cholent*
36. Ashkelon to Hebron (dir.)
38. Classifieds
39. Jamie Lee Curtis
40. Hamantasch
42. Conquerors of Israel
44. *Zetz* (English)
45. Switch positions
47. Sukkah

48. Jody Scheckter's need
50. Dances
51. Astronomer
52. Alenu action
53. Al Jolson position
54. Little bit
55. Freud invention
56. Blessed every 28 years
58. Einstein activity
60. Commandment
61. Gaza to Jerusalem (dir.)

Puzzle 30

Across

1. Jacob after the angel
5. Kosher hooves
10. __ *Gadya*
14. Son of Gad
15. Moses on the mount
16. Not on *Shabbat*
17. Eden sound
18. Desert food
19. Esther's kingdom?
20. Cheer
21. Emulated the *Chazzan*
22. Rhea Perlman's sitcom
24. Cosmetic mogul
26. Political party
27. Israeli army
29. Hebrew letter
30. Ahava product
33. Composer Copland
34. *Mezuzot* sites
35. Ashdod to Jericho (dir.)
36. Killed biblically
37. Qumran features
38. 1,003
39. __ *Rungs*, Buber
40. Targets for Alcott
41. Haifa, Eilat, and Ashdod
42. *Mems* (English)
43. Angel of Death path
44. Moses' cradle
45. Raised
46. Italian *varnishkes*
47. Author Jacqueline
50. Dreidel features?
51. *Chazzer* (English)
54. Sabin vaccine "oral"
55. Moses' bush
57. Identical
58. __ *18*, Uris novel
59. Potok specialty
60. Issachar city
61. Valley (Hebrew)
62. Samson's strength
63. Japanese *shekelim*

Down

1. Cowardly Lion actor
2. Jan Peerce piece
3. Current Defense minister
4. Cantor and Goldman
5. Writer Maurice
6. Craft for Arkia
7. Nazarite hair
8. King David__, Jerusalem
9. Rabbis
10. *Shivah* sounds
11. Employ
12. Purim month
13. Lion's lairs
21. Jazzman Getz
23. *Streimels*
25. Sid Ceasar's __ *of Shows*
26. Teva offering
27. Agam specialty
28. Old Jerusalem?
29. Lid
30. JDL founder
31. Join

32. Abraham was the first
34. Fourth letter of Alephbet
37. *Bris*
38. Greatest
40. Shofar
41. *Mitla* ___, Uris novel
44. Jewish doughnuts?
45. Balaam's boss?
46. Shimon

47. A few
48. "A Priest with __ and Thummim"
49. Transaction
50. Breathing
52. Noah's rainbow
53. Eilat stones
56. Pro
57. Speak

1	2	3	4		5	6	7	8	9		10	11	12	13
14					15						16			
17					18						19			
20				21					22	23				
		24	25					26						
27	28						29					30	31	32
33						34						35		
36					37						38			
39				40						41				
42				43					44					
			45					46						
47	48	49					50					51	52	53
54					55	56					57			
58					59						60			
61					62						63			

Puzzle 31

Across

1. Lighten
5. Lawgiver
10. Cantor and Goldman
13. Expert
14. Make *aliyah*
15. Three: comb. form
16. Giant Dead Sea tribe
17. Solomon's secret
18. Cane for Moses
19. Leah's third
20. Minor Prophet
21. Raphael's haunt
23. Lee J. Cobb role
25. Graven__
26. Haman's fifth
29. Magic Carpet base
30. Bar Kochba
31. Empire over Israel
33. Imitated Chaim Gross
37. __ Aviv
38. Via Maris

41. Ithamar high priest
42. Hurried
44. Ender
45. Noah's milieu
47. Gabbai catch
49. *Varnishkes*
50. *Havdalah* odors
53. Forty days for Noah
55. Tsahal vehicles
56. Emcee Parks
57. Naomi at times
61. __ *carte*
62. Israeli wood
64. Jewish calendar
65. Commandments
66. Coats
67. __ *Hall*, Allen film
68. Evil__
69. Landers and Van Buren
70. *Mitzvah*, good __

Down

1. Reputation
2. Spring (Hebrew)
3. Director Cecil
4. *Nuns* (English)
5. Leah to Issachar
6. Sight for Sagan
7. Hebrew letters
8. Haifa to Nazareth (dir.)
9. Tahina
10. Lulav companion
11. Imitated Paul Newman
12. Four to a dreidel

13. Radioman Allen
20. Sabin's organization
22. Klezmatics
24. Chanukah need
25. Einstein specialty
26. Shaw and Shamsky
27. Jonah's milieu
28. Competent
29. King of Judah
31. Sacrifices
32. Solomon's find
34. Moses' camouflage

35. Security experts
36. Kiddush drink
39. *Hamantaschen*
40. Mezuzah holder
43. Canasta need
46. Kibbutz
48. Engedi
49. Never
50. Israel in 1948
51. CBS exec.
52. *Meshugge* (English)
53. Days of creation
54. Delilah cut Samson's
56. Netenyahu nickname
58. Diary author
59. Entebbe Operation
60. Exist
63. *Shiva* mood
64. *Yeled* (English)

Puzzle 32

Across

1. Great tenor Peerce
4. Alias
7. Hebrew letter
10. Dues
13. Son of Gad
14. Scrip
15. __ mode
16. Anger
17. Wailing Wall today
19. Miriam's instrument
21. King of Israel
22. *Chuppah* holder
24. Sculptor's style
25. Ancestry
26. Whichever
27. *Charoset*
30. __ *Kapital*, Marx work
32. Al Rosen stat.
34. Skillful
35. *Cosmos* author
38. Organizations for Koufax
40. Methuselah
41. El-Al posting
42. Mother (Hebrew)
44. *Maude* star
45. Edom people
46. Rickles
47. Actress Pinchon
49. "Baby Snooks"
51. Bomber (abbr.)
53. Prophesize
54. Emulated Deborah
55. Engedi
57. Third king of Judah
59. Writer Sholem
63. Digit
64. Garden
65. __ *18*, Uris novel
66. Israeli coins
69. Lou Grant actor
71. *Hamantasch*
72. Karpas ritual
73. Bilhah's boy
74. Travel club
75. Rosen and Jolson
76. Jonathan Pollard?
77. Blessed every 28 years
78. King David?

Down

1. Eilat stone
2. Son of Gad
3. First month?
4. Ribicoff
5. Bitter herbs
6. Writer
7. Adam to Eve
8. Wallach
9. Aurthur Murray step
10. Plague victim
11. In front of
12. *Treif* wiggler
18. Actress (with 20 down)
20. Actress (with 18 down)
23. David's instument
27. Marceau
28. Woody or Mel
29. Singer Helen

31. Issachar city
33. *Rosemary's* __, Levin novel
35. Order
36. Say the Viddui
37. The Stick and Dandy Phil
38. *Agadah*
39. Snug
43. Greatest
48. Imitate Moses
50. *Get Smart* guy
52. Piece for Fischer

54. *Mission Impossible* star
56. Moses camouflage
58. *Hamantaschen* filling
60. Commandment site
61. Pesach preparation
62. Abraham's brother
64. View
66. Via Maris, "__ Road"
67. *Barney Miller*'s Linden
68. Rim
70. Columnist Landers

1	2	3	■	4	5	6	■	7	8	9	■	10	11	12
13			■	14			■	15			■	16		
17			18				■	19			20			
21				■	22		23		■	24			■	■
25				■	26			■	27				28	29
■	■		30	31		■	32	33		■	34			
35	36	37			■	38			■	39	■	40		
41			■	42	43		■	44			■	45		
46			■	47		■	48		■	49	50			
51			52		53			■	54			■	■	■
55				56		■	57	58			59	60	61	62
■		63			■	64					65			
66	67				68		■	69		70				
71			■	72			■	73			■	74		
75			■	76			■	77			■	78		

Puzzle 33

Across

1. Make the Golden Calf
5. PLO member
9. Li'l __, Capp cartoon
14. Jan Peerce piece
15. Amy Alcott target
16. Sculptor Elkan
17. *Chutzpa* (English)
18. Israeli city
19. Lineage
20. Jamie __ Curtis
22. Comedian Harvey
24. Standing prayer
27. Title for Jacob Epstein
28. Four to a dreidel
32. Girl's name
33. Maccabiah game
35. *Seinfeld* or *The Nanny*
37. Baer's milieu
39. Nazarite hair
41. Samuel and Amos
42. Principles signing city
44. Samson's triumphant site
46. Uncle Miltie
49. Broke the ninth commandment
51. Resnik's organization
55. Tales (Hebrew)
57. Pomegranate plenty
59. *Yeled* (English)
60. Columnist Barrett
61. Greenberg stat.
63. Sabra
65. Temple site
68. Scrip
69. Hebrew letter
72. *Vavs* (English)
74. Noah before his sons
77. Activist Hoffman
78. Israeli Valley
79. Ancestry
80. Sukkot decorations
81. Not on *Shabbat*
82. Security experts

Down

1. Jerry Lewis specialty
2. Levin
3. *Pentimento* author Hellman
4. Fourth letter of Alephbet
5. Got ya!
6. __ *of Ages*
7. Baseball player "Flip"
8. Negev kibbutz
9. Former Israeli minister
10. Conductor
11. Jerusalem to Tiberias (dir.)
12. Gaza to Jerusalem (dir.)
13. Actor Steiger
21. *Hamantasch*
23. Title for Golda
24. El-Al milieu
25. 1,501
26. Deal maker Monty
29. __ man, Doron Sheffer
30. Israelite city
31. *Mems* (English)
34. Mt. Hermon climate

36. Sort of? (ending)
38. Former Israeli Prime Minister
40. *Simcha*
43. Mediterranean
45. Paradise
46. __ Kochba revolt
47. Freud invention
48. Like David from Saul
50. Afula Citizen
52. Columnist Van Buren
53. Spin (Hebrew)
54. Heschel to friends

56. That one
58. Little bit
62. Nile
64. Seder locale
66. Bialik writings
67. *Rosh* (English)
69. Round for Spitz
70. Vigoda
71. Degree
73. That woman
75. Genetic messenger
76. Wiggling *treif* fish

1	2	3	4		5	6	7	8		9	10	11	12	13
14					15					16				
17					18					19				
	20		21		22		23							
24	25				26		27				28	29	30	31
32				33		34			35	36				
37			38		39			40		41				
		42	43				44	45						
46	47	48				49	50				51	52	53	54
55				56		57			58		59			
60					61	62			63		64			
		65	66				67		68					
69	70	71				72			73		74		75	76
77					78						79			
80					81						82			

Puzzle 34

Across

1. Haifa
4. Sally J. Priesand
9. Maccabiah event
13. Dance
14. Assumed name
15. Former Israeli ambassador
16. Sinai climate
17. Torah portion
18. Nebbish?
19. Freud inventions
20. Her
21. Capital of Goshen
23. Sukkot activity
26. Jody Scheckter's need
27. Make *aliyah*
28. Used his *tuches*
30. Sabras
34. *Hamantasch*
36. Gottex suit top
38. Rothschild business?
39. Ever to Emma Lazarus
42. Emulated Moses
44. Literary initials

46. Dreidel letter
47. Jazzman Getz
49. Elie Wiesel novel
51. Travel club
53. Synagogue
55. Peace __, political organization
57. Political party
61. Matriarchs
63. Actress Kahn
65. Day of rest
69. Gives a horn?
70. 52
71. *Zaftig* (English)
72. Edna Ferber novel
74. Murray and Shamsky
75. Hebrew month
76. Lauder
77. "The New Colossus"
78. Hebrew letters
79. Sukkot
80. *Alenu*

Down

1. Line with Jordan
2. Haman's eighth
3. Torah pointer (Hebrew)
4. Torah commentator
5. Non-Hebrew tribes
6. Offering
7. Comedienne Roseanne
8. Stern or Asimov
9. Moshe Dayan
10. Ribicoff and Vigoda

11. Mount for Mordecai
12. *Tsitsit* sites
13. Israeli port city
20. Break the eighth commandment
22. Apple computer
24. Ashdod to Be'er Sheba (dir.)
25. *Schmooz* (English)
29. Three: comb. form

31. Jonathan Pollard?
32. Zeta Beta ___, fraternity
33. King David__, Jerusalem
35. Comic Buttons
37. Dershowitz organization?
39. Eat (Yiddish)
40. And others (abbr.)
41. Cheer
43. Bilhah's boy
45. Old Jerusalem?
48. Bible book
50. __ Kippur
52. Named in a *Mishaberach*

54. Sabin's milieu
56. Sounded the shofar
58. Jerusalem valley
59. UJA word
60. Abraham's belief
62. Prophets
64. Sukkah decorations?
65. Emulated Spitz
66. *Afikoman* action
67. Man (Hebrew)
68. Table (Yiddish)
73. Enjoyed *manna*
74. Monkey

Puzzle 35

Across

1. Brother to Japheth
4. Vigoda and Heschel
8. Singer Lawrence
13. Freud invention
14. Head (Hebrew)
15. George Burns trademark
16. Thou
17. Anne Frank's dad
18. Arkia shed
19. Nibble (Yiddish)
21. Tired
23. Give a tenth
25. Monty Hall specialties
26. *Schmooz* (English)
29. Uzis
30. Simeon
31. Deli fare listing
32. *Joys of Yiddish* author __ Rosten
33. Not on *Pesach*
34. Goodman
35. Chants Torah

37. Jonah's prison
39. Imitated Moe Berg?
41. Make *havdalah* candles
43. Owns
46. Hermon or Masada
47. *Machers*
48. Plague
49. Slang affirmation
50. "Great" king of Judea
51. Sabras
52. Leah's Dad
53. New day?
54. Negev
57. Purim month
59. Ten make a *minyan*
62. *Bimahs*
63. Circumcision
64. "Friend" to Montand
65. Anne's story
66. *Daleds* (English)
67. *Shluf* (English)

Down

1. Hebrew letter
2. Long before
3. Temple site (2 words)
4. Made *aliyah*
5. Two included
6. Hester Street time zone
7. Forty day forecast
8. Seen at the Sukkah
9. Curtis
10. Roasted on *Pesach*
11. __Maris, Jerusalem

12. Ever to Emma Lazarus
15. Commandment word
20. Expressions of ease
22. Tel Aviv to Jerusalem (dir.)
23. Prayer for dew
24. Anger
25. Out of Israel
26. *The French Connection* star
27. Columnist Landers
28. Purchase
30. Satiated

31. Actor Brooks
33. Hand (Hebrew)
34. Hammerin' Hank's tool
36. Scream
38. ___ *tadrut*
39. Jonathan Pollard?
40. Not on *Pesach?*
42. Conducter Bernstein
44. Chagall genre
45. Mt. Hermon activity
47. Usurous vehicles

48. ___ *Kapital,* Marx work
50. Houdini
51. Chicken soups?
52. Producer Norman
53. Israeli fruit
54. Jacob to Zebulun
55. Ithamar high priest
56. Depot (abbr.)
58. Reason for *shiva*
60. Mother (Hebrew)
61. *Shikker*'s sip

Puzzle 36

Across

1. Expressions of ease
4. Makes a *fey* a *pey*
7. Hebrew letter
10. Often to Nelly Sachs
13. Genesis starter
14. Jonas Salk's organization
15. ___ *carte*
16. Title for Jacob Epstein
17. Storage city
19. Chanukah story
21. One for Roberta Peters
22. Emma Lazarus gift
24. Cass Elliott
25. *Av* or *Tammuz*
27. Secular
28. Simeon
29. Lubavitcher
31. Divan
32. Son to Jacob
35. 2,105
36. Torah chanter
40. Hebrew letter
42. Dead Sea cosmetics
44. Dance
45. Israeli measures
47. Like *shiva* clothes
49. Hirsch to friends
50. *Noodge* (English)
51. Son of Ishmael
53. Ellis and Staten
56. Satiated
57. Hebrew letter
61. *Tefillin* letter
62. David Frye *schtick*
64. Fighter Rosenblatt
65. Chanakah must
67. UJA tour
69. Exist
70. Ellis Isle time zone
71. Tis, to Nelly Sachs
72. 700
73. ___ *tadrut*
74. *Sin* (English)
75. Pastrami on ___
76. Her

Down

1. Abraham once
2. *Shema* starter (2 words)
3. Passover sign
4. __ *Kapital,* Marx work
5. Tenth part of an *ephah*
6. Tossing crumbs
7. Al Jolson hit
8. *Night* author
9. Damage
10. Award for Dustin Hoffman
11. Woody Allen specialty
12. *Nosh* (English)
18. Einstein's specialty
20. Standing prayer
23. Holocaust memorial
26. Son to Noah
28. Dues
30. *Potch* (English)
31. *Havdalah* candle
32. Dike

33. *Shikker*'s choice
34. Biblical fishing device
37. David O. Selznick
38. Bo Belinsky stat.
39. Shofar source
41. Chavurah member
43. Horowitz
46. Taxmen
48. Prayer for dew
52. Patriarchs
53. Sis to Lot and Milcah
54. Puppeteer Lewis

55. Speech in Simon production
56. Max Baer's weapons
58. Zilpah and Bilhah
59. Methuselah's dad
60. *Hora*
62. *Mishmash* (English)
63. Avdat or Eilat
66. Actor Cobb
68. Ashdod to Be'er Sheva (dir.)

Puzzle 37

Across

1. Greatest
5. Acted the *shikker*
10. Jonas Salk's organization
13. Buried at Machpelah
14. Biblical judge
15. *Meshugge* (English)
16. Hebrew letter
17. Kol__
18. Title for Golda
19. Emulate Klugman
20. And others (abbr.)
22. Ehud Olmert
24. Fiddler's location
26. Negev condition
29. Israeli land measure
31. Israeli flag feature
33. Karpas ritual
35. Seder action
36. *Feh*
37. Seth's boy
39. Digit
40. Often to Bialik
43. Kol Nidre sound

45. Affirmative
46. Ellis Island time zone
47. Amy Alcott's score
48. Imitated Mauri Rose
50. *Mikveh*
52. Month
54. "Water" to Marcel Marceau
55. Passover guest
59. Items on Schindler's list
61. *Chatchkes* (English)
63. Actress Theda
64. Feather, candle, and __
66. Ashkelon to Hebron (dir.)
68. Hebrew letter
69. Her
70. Adam to Seth
73. Moses' bush
75. Used his *tuches*
76. Righteous Schindler
77. Beelzebub
78. *Sin* (English)
79. Zilpah and Bilhah
80. Mizrach location

Down

1. MGM lion
2. Abba Eban
3. Tisha B'av mood
4. You, biblically
5. Arthur Murray milieu
6. Sid Gordon's stat.
7. Einstein action
8. Lear to his friends
9. Make challah
10. Lot's progeny

11. Conversos
12. Classifieds
13. Seen at the Sukkah
21. *Hatikvah*
23. Jew (Yiddish)
25. Commandment no no
27. Fruit drink
28. K'Tonton
30. Encounter
32. *Mitla* __, Uris novel

34. Dorothy Parker
38. Bellow or Raskin
40. Exposed
41. Black Jews
42. Shofars?
44. Buddy Rich specialty
49. Simon and Garfunkel
51. Baby's cover
53. Rabbi __ Baeck
56. U.S. Senator (R-NY)

57. Ark's end
58. Nod to Cain
60. Home to Lot
62. 50 to the Jubilee
65. Resnik's organization
67. Seder manner
69. Gaza to Be'er Sheva (dir.)
71. 601
72. Jacob to Judah
74. Air organization

Puzzle 38

Across

1. Ribicoff and Vigoda
5. Pointers
9. Monty Hall specialties
14. Cease
15. Victim of Zimri
16. Israeli city
17. Month before Nisan
18. Sandal maker
19. Be'er __
20. Woody Allen film
22. *Shmutz* (English)
24. Biblical fishing device
25. Abraham to Midian
27. Reason for *shiva*
28. The Golden __
29. Guitarist Dylan
32. Nickname for Salk
34. Ponder
36. Street (abbr.)
37. Jewish restaurant
39. Sinai ship?
43. U. S. Supreme Court Justice

47. Witch's dwelling
48. Codifier Joseph
49. Baseball's Shamsky
50. Sixth day creation
53. *Bubkes* (English)
54. __ relief, sculptor's style
55. Actress Madeline
58. Torah breastplate
60. Rosen and Arkin
62. *Shikker*'s choice?
63. Passion
65. Cane for Moses
69. Step
71. Freud inventions
73. Israeli mountain
74. Houdini
75. Resnik's organization
76. Competent
77. Made *aliyah*
78. Killed biblically
79. Kinneret

Down

1. Eleventh king of Judah
2. Called biblically
3. On High (Hebrew)
4. Gaza __
5. Soon
6. Hebrew letter
7. Brubeck or Brenner
8. Greeting
9. Maccabiah race
10. Number ending
11. Concluding prayer

12. Blood __
13. Israel in 1948
21. Actress Paulette
23. Zeta Beta ___, fraternity
26. Ginsberg specialty
28. Chant Torah
29. Moses in the bullrushes
30. Challah maker's equipment
31. *Alenu* action
33. 151
35. Torahs

38. Corp.
40. Lot's son-in-law
41. Prophet of synagogues
42. "Purim" or cast __
44. Comedian Rivers
45. Container
46. One for Bubbles?
51. Enjoyed manna
52. Experts
55. Buckwheat groats
56. Bimah

57. *Shema* starter (2 words)
59. *Love Story* author
61. Act the *gonif*
63. Mime David
64. "The __," Midler's movie
66. Father (Hebrew)
67. *Columbo* star
68. Exodus
70. Taxmen
72. Prophesized

1	2	3	4		5	6	7	8		9	10	11	12	13
14					15					16				
17					18					19				
20				21		22			23			24		
			25		26		27				28			
29	30	31		32		33		34		35				
36				37			38			39		40	41	42
43			44					45	46					
47						48					49			
			50		51	52		53				54		
55	56	57			58		59		60		61			
62				63				64		65		66	67	68
69			70			71			72		73			
74					75						76			
77					78						79			

Puzzle 39

Across

1. Organization for Bugsy Siegel
4. Dike
7. *Schmooz* (English)
10. Canaanite or Amorite
13. __ *Maamin,* Wiesel novel
14. Baseball's Shamsky
15. __ carte
16. Fruit drink
17. First Kibbutz
19. Baal Tekiah
21. Spielberg's Schindler
22. *Greps* (English)
23. Give a tenth
25. Actor Arkin
27. Chant Torah
30. Johnny Kling stat.
31. Sarah (formerly)
33. Pianist Victor
34. *Happy* __ Winkler sitcom
36. Adam to Seth
37. The Jazz Singer
38. Many-colored
40. Imitate Mark Roth
41. Bath-sheba to Solomon
44. Existed
45. *Sov* (Hebrew)
49. Gabbai catch
50. Joyce Brothers alias
52. Al Rosen stat.
53. Not on Yom Kippur
54. Bacharach
55. Rainbows
57. Betim in Spain
59. Ellis and Staten
61. Love, honor, and __
63. Actor Peter
66. Mauri Rose need
67. *Daled* (English)
68. Herman Barron need
69. *Shluf* (English)
70. Platters by Bolton
71. *Sin* (English)
72. Math word
73. Thou possessive

Down

1. *Meshugge* (English)
2. *Echad* (English)
3. ADL fight
4. Horas
5. One for Jan Peerce
6. Ark landing site (2 words)
7. Torah attendant
8. Woody or Mel
9. Pagan sun god
10. Patriarchs
11. Judah Ha-Levi specialty
12. Ever to Bialik
18. Biblical sign of mourning
20. Torahs
23. Koppel
24. Author Levin
26. *Yeled* (English)
28. Long before
29. Daniel's test site
32. Month after Shevat

33. Ark front
35. Yeshiva member
37. Baseball player with 40 down
39. Over to Bialik
40. Baseball player with 37 down
41. Hebrew letter
42. Solomon's mine product
43. Genealogists
44. Jihad, Holy __
46. Chanukah *gelt*
47. Son of (Sephardic)

48. 100 *agarot*
50. Shrubs
51. Closed the Torah
54. Hubs for Tsahal
56. Actor Brooks
58. Four to a dreidel
60. Pomegranate plenty
61. Gideon's best men
62. Owned
64. Cheer
65. Jonathan Pollard

1	2	3		4	5	6		7	8	9		10	11	12
13				14				15				16		
17			18					19			20			
		21						22						
23	24					25	26				27		28	29
30				31	32				33					
34			35		36				37					
		38	39				40							
41	42	43					44				45	46	47	48
49					50				51		52			
53					54				55	56				
		57		58				59	60					
61	62							63					64	65
66				67				68				69		
70				71				72				73		

Puzzle 40

Across

1. Number ending
4. Used his *tuches*
7. Zimram to Abraham
10. Capp and Jolson
13. To and __
14. "Friend" to Wiesel
15. Mother (Hebrew)
16. Tsahal graduate
17. Comedian Marty
19. Shamsky was one
20. Freud invention
21. Amos and Isaiah
22. Moses' bush
24. Daniel's test locale
25. Kol Nidre sound
27. __ a boy!
28. Samson's weapon
29. Meadow
32. Kol__
34. Prepares *shiva* garments
35. One for Roberta Peters
37. Matriarchs
38. Degree
39. *Yentl*, star

45. *Feh*
46. Haman or Amalek
47. Tried and __
48. Judah ha-Levi homeland
51. Idolator
53. Gaza to Jerusalem (dir.)
54. "Abba" to Marceau
55. Dinah to Simeon
56. David O. Selznick
58. Son of Gad
59. Be'er Sheva region
61. Dead Sea plenty
65. *Sin* (English)
66. B'nai B'rith organization
67. Hagar's son
69. American Mossad?
70. Prophesize
71. Evil __
72. K'Tonton
73. Israeli conquest
74. Fiedler to friends
75. Yom Kippur or Gulf
76. Tiberias to Tel Aviv (dir.)

Down

1. *Fays* (English)
2. Life or Knowledge
3. Barron aim
4. Delilah's guy
5. Jonas Salk's organization
6. *Gilligan's Island* actress
7. Hebrew ancestor
8. Measurements
9. Sharansky to friends

10. Photographer Richard
11. *Agadah* (English)
12. David's ammo
18. Salk and Sabin
23. Greenberg's position
26. Altar (Hebrew)
28. *Beheyme* (English)
29. Sabin's milieu
30. Byzantine or Messianic

31. El-Al milieu
33. —*Kapital,* Marx work
34. Al Rosen stat.
36. Activist Hoffman
38. Prophesizing elder
40. Copeland on track
41. *Shmatah* (English)
42. Exist
43. Dreidel letter
44. *Daled* (English)
48. Abba Eban specialty
49. Kingdom of Ahasuerus

50. Haman's eighth
51. Baby *chazzer*
52. Nibbler (Yiddish)
55. Order
57. Goldwyn to friends
59. Resnik's organization
60. Observe
62. Ten commandments
63. Amy Alcott needs
64. Killed biblically
68. Literary initials

1	2	3		4	5	6		7	8	9		10	11	12
13				14				15				16		
17			18					19				20		
21						22	23					24		
			25		26		27				28			
29	30	31		32		33				34				
35			36		37				38					
39				40				41				42	43	44
			45				46				47			
48	49	50				51				52		53		
54					55			56		57				
58				59				60		61		62	63	64
65				66				67	68					
69				70				71				72		
73				74				75				76		

Puzzle 41

Across

1. Preminger
5. Purim month (Hebrew)
9. Purim villain
14. Pesach herbs?
15. Actress Theda
16. Israeli coin
17. Chicken soup?
18. Night before (Hebrew)
19. The waters of __
20. Boat for Noah
21. Imitate the "four sons"?
22. Mother (Hebrew)
24. Alphabet run
25. Baseball MVP Al
27. *Meshugge* (English)
29. Stairs
32. Segaloff or Stone
36. Amish look-alikes?
39. Sage Eiger
40. Son to Noah
41. Haifa to Hebron (dir.)
42. __*Kapital,* Marx work
44. 52
45. Say the Viddui
47. Journalist Walter
49. Strauss jeans
51. Son of Aaron
52. False witnesses
54. Bert Parks
58. Alien craft?
61. Zilpah's sons
62. Jonathan Pollard?
64. Third king of Judah
65. Torah commentator
67. Gilead medicine
69. Observes *shiva*
70. Ellis and Staten
71. *Dawn* author
72. Life or Knowledge
73. Forty days for Noah
74. Edomite mountain
75. Joel (Hebrew)

Down

1. Award for Streisand
2. Rhode Island synagogue
3. Ottoman Empire
4. Solomon's mine find
5. Vigoda and Heschel
6. Plague
7. Exist
8. Noah's messenger
9. Haman's ears
10. Golden __ of Spain
11. Artist Chagall
12. Son of Gad
13. Item on Schindler's list
21. Nazi practice
23. Matriarchs
26. Eat (Yiddish)
27. Belief: comb. form
28. Scream
30. Cantor and Goldman
31. Soupy's ammo
33. Depraved
34. *Fear No __,* Sharansky work
35. Yael's weapon
36. __*Gadya*

37. Bigot's forte
38. King of Judah
42. 504
43. ___ *Maamin,* Wiesel novel
46. *Bubkes* (English)
47. Existed
48. Purr
50. Prophesized
53. Biblical garb
55. Egyptian capital

56. Cosmetic mogul
57. Equipment for Baskin
58. *The Angry Hills* author
59. Writer Howard
60. Accords city
62. 152
63. Lag B' ___
66. That one
68. *Shikker's* choice
69. *Chazzer* house

Puzzle 42

Across

1. Neil Simon specialty
5. Li'l Abner creator
9. Codifier
13. Pierced as sign of bondsmen
15. Skillful
16. King of Judah
17. *Eretz* (English)
18. Race-car driver
20. Tay-Sachs carrier
21. Imitate
23. "Sea" to Wiesel
24. Golden rule
25. Eilat stone
26. Actress Theda
28. Pouch
30. Cantor and Goldman
31. Imps
33. Prayer starts, "Hear O"
37. Existed
38. __ *Crowd*, Birmingham
40. Esther's kingdom?
41. American spy
46. Magic Carpet source
47. *Shikker*'s choice
48. *Meshugge* (English)
49. *Beaches* actress
51. Nazi race
53. Noah to Ham
56. Depot (abbr.)
58. Negev particle
59. Exist
60. Finance degree
63. B'nai B'rith organization
65. Haifa to Jerusalem (dir.)
66. Israeli coin
67. Zilpah and Bilhah
70. *Hagba'ah*
72. Author Ferber
73. 2,002
74. Nazarite no no
75. Herman Barron need
76. Joel or Amos
77. Like *shiva* clothes

Down

1. UJA promise
2. Acted the Usurer
3. Baseball player Cal
4. Soon
5. Vishniac equipment
6. Nizer organization
7. Fruit for slivovitz
8. Former Israeli Prime Minister
9. Need for 18 across
10. Writer Oz
11. Zionist Halprin
12. ___ *Shabbat*
14. "The Bride"
19. Gershwin and Morris
22. Weekly *sidra*
27. *Kol Nidre* chanters
29. Pre-Bar Mitzvah?
32. Enjoy cholent
34. Koufax stat.
35. Damage
36. *I __ Thou*, Martin Buber

37. Covets
39. Vishniac and Polanski
41. Baer move
42. Ha-Levi specialty
43. Biblical fishing device
44. __ *mode*
45. Dear Abby's sister
50. Village of Simeon
52. PLO leader
53. Great prophet

54. Haman's eighth
55. Sinai
57. Gimbel and Sandler
60. Hebrew letter
61. Lighten
62. Diary writer Frank
64. Etrog's cousin
68. __*Kapital*, Marx work
69. Reason for *shiva*
71. Sighs

Puzzle 43

Across

1. *Gadol* (English)
4. Arafat's organization
7. Torah breastplate
10. Title for Montefiore
13. Fruit drink
14. Arkia milieu
15. Alphabet run
16. Movie channel
17. Cardozo to friends
18. *Shmatah* (English)
19. Yiddish disdain
20. B'nai B'rith youth organization
21. Israeli Olympian
24. Cacti
26. Divan
27. Hebrew letter
29. Sopher specialty
30. Challahs
33. Israeli airline
35. King of Israel
36. More sacred
38. Little bit
41. Over to Bialik
42. Generation (Hebrew)
43. Issachar to Levi
44. *Shema* ender
45. Nizer pleasure
46. Nomad
48. Tsahal need
49. *Beaches* star
50. Graven__
52. Desert cool spots
55. Bo Belinsky stat.
57. Number ending
58. Rabbi specialty
60. Presented at Nuremberg
64. Ever to Emma Lazarus
65. Evil eye
67. Acted
68. Vase
69. Genetic messenger
70. Son of Gad
71. Named in a *Mishaberach*
72. Good (Hebrew)
73. Sacrifice residue
74. Scheinblum stat.
75. Gelilah act
76. Jonathan Pollard?

Down

1. *Rosemary's* __, Levin novel
2. Einstein specialty
3. *Bat Masterson*, star
4. *Adalyadah*
5. False Witness
6. Pipes
7. Hebrew letter
8. Ribicoff and Vigoda
9. Kosher wine maker
10. Puppeteer Lewis
11. Biblical judge
12. Prepare Seder egg
22. Strauss
23. Monty Hall specialty
25. Top for Gottex
28. Asherites or Gadites

30. Commandment no no
31. Tenth part of an ephah
32. Use an Uzi
34. Olympian Strug
37. Emulate Abba Eban
38. Israeli Chanukah sweets
39. Frank
40. First Jewish Miss America
42. *The Nanny* star
47. Slight bit
48. Dung or Jaffa

49. Golden girl Arthur
51. Act the *yenta*
52. Roberta Peters genre
53. Defense minister Moshe
54. Asher's daughter
56. Israeli city
59. ___ Alpert, bandleader
61. Matriarchs
62. *Spelt*
63. Coveting
66. Tribes

1	2	3		4	5	6		7	8	9		10	11	12
13				14				15				16		
17				18				19				20		
21			22				23		24		25			
		26				27		28		29				
30	31				32		33		34					
35					36	37						38	39	40
41				42				43				44		
45				46			47				48			
			49						50	51				
52	53	54				55		56		57				
58					59		60		61				62	63
64				65		66		67				68		
69				70				71				72		
73				74				75				76		

Puzzle 44

Across

1. Rubin or Bronfman
4. __ *carte*
7. Jerusalem to Ashkelon (dir.)
10. *Pisk* (Yiddish)
13. "Lands of the Covenant"
14. Israelite city
15. __ Man, Doron Sheffer
16. Solomon's find
17. Newswoman Walters
19. Baseball's Art
21. Scout
22. Edom nobles
23. Negev kibbutz
25. Pagan deity
27. *Tzedakah* purpose
30. Bo Belinsky stat.
31. Shofar blast
33. Woman of ___
34. Buddy Rich instrument
36. Whichever
37. High priests?
38. Dreidels
40. Writer Irving
41. Moses' bush
44. Sound of awe
45. 2,600
49. Sage Akiva
50. Gracie's hubby George
52. El-Al milieu
53. *Shema* starter
54. *Shikker*s (English)
55. CBS exec.
57. Sacrifices often
59. David's guard
61. Mossad
63. Chanukah story
66. Rest on *tuches*
67. Judah to Zebulun
68. "Friend" to Wiesel
69. *Treif* meat cut
70. Ashdod to Jericho
71. Columnist Landers
72. Biblical fishing device
73. Girl's name

Down

1. Vessel for Rickover
2. Third king of Judah
3. French mime
4. Haman's fifth
5. Agadah
6. Israeli neighbors
7. Solomon's gift
8. Synagogue
9. Frail
10. Cantor Rosenblatt
11. Torah sanctuary
12. Israeli dreidel letter
18. __ Kochba revolt
20. President Begin
23. Divan
24. Johnny Kling stat.
26. Negev climate
28. Long period
29. Freud and Sabin
32. Rounds for Spitz

33. Taken under a *chupah*
35. Israeli peak
37. Founder of Paramount Pictures
39. Over to Bialik
40. Mordecai through Shushan
41. Yiddish disdain
42. Bear false witness
43. Haman's tribe
44. Three strikes for Rosen
46. Prophet of the return
47. Reason for *shiva*

48. *Battle ___*, Uris novel
50. Fiedler's Pops locale
51. Lilith
54. Violinist Isaac
56. Alias
58. Father (Hebrew)
60. Etrog's cousin
61. Haifa to Hebron (dir.)
62. Biblical measure
64. *Yeled* (English)
65. Mother (Hebrew)

1	2	3		4	5	6		7	8	9		10	11	12
13				14				15				16		
17			18					19			20			
		21						22						
23	24					25	26				27		28	29
30				31	32					33				
34			35		36				37					
			38	39				40						
41	42	43					44				45	46	47	48
49						50				51		52		
53					54					55	56			
		57		58				59	60					
61	62							63					64	65
66				67				68				69		
70				71				72				73		

Puzzle 45

Across

1. Kunstler organization
4. Be'ersheba to Jerusalem (dir.)
7. Torah breastplate
10. *Shmatah* (English)
13. Blessed every 28 years
14. Dreidel
15. B.C.E. word
16. Long before
17. *Zetz* (English)
18. Sound of laughter
19. *Bissel* (English)
20. Avdat to Ashdod (dir.)
21. *Night* author
23. *Chazzar*
25. Leviathan
27. Forty days for Noah
29. __*Kapital*, Marx work
31. Defense minister, Moshe
32. Baby holder
34. "The New Colossus"
36. Sort of? (ending)
38. Jael's victim
40. David's instrument
44. Resnik's ride

46. Joseph's readings
48. *Mishmash* (English)
49. Issachar city
51. Zilpah and Rachel
52. Tent for Abraham
54. *Mizrach* location?
56. Oasis offering
59. Tisha B'av mood
61. Shavuot (English)
64. Greenberg specialties
66. Dike
68. "Star __," Nimoy's series
69. "Water" to Elie Wiesel
70. Airport locale
72. Winger to friends
74. Geller
75. Title for Golda
76. Anger
77. *Daled* (English)
78. Exist
79. Vote yes
80. NIS word
81. Alias
82. ___*tadrut*

Down

1. Sacrifice residue
2. Emulated Herod
3. "Madman" to Maccabees
4. Last degree
5. Father of Ham
6. High priest vestment
7. Koppel
8. Israeli city

9. Cacti
10. Extent
11. Writer
12. Worn under chupahs
22. Sid Gordon stat.
24. Tithed
26. Son of Gad
28. Drizzle

30. Join Tsahal
33. Silvers role
35. Hagba'ah
36. Belief: comb. form
37. That woman
39. *Hamantaschen* filling
41. Yom Kippur (Hebrew)
42. Tay-Sachs carrier
43. *Sin* (English)
45. Hebrew letter
47. Bandleader Artie
50. Salty sea

53. Irving
55. *Tefillin*
56. Prayer starts, "Hear O"
57. Methuselah
58. Dangerfield's hope
60. Jacob to Gad
62. Olympian Strug
63. El-Al milieu
65. Ache
67. Lamb-like
71. Tal hope
73. Golden girl Arthur

1	2	3		4	5	6		7	8	9		10	11	12
13				14				15				16		
17				18				19				20		
21			22		23		24		25		26			
27			28			29		30		31				
	32			33			34		35					
36	37			38		39					40	41	42	43
44			45					46		47				
48					49		50				51			
		52	53					54		55				
56	57	58				59		60		61			62	63
64				65		66		67		68				
69			70		71		72		73		74			
75			76				77				78			
79			80				81				82			

Puzzle 46

Across

1. Make the Mandelbread
5. *Wizard of Oz* lion
9. Terrorists
14. Arkin or King
15. One for Bubbles?
16. Fromm or Segal
17. Ramat Gan specialty
18. Rachel's resting place
19. Kill biblically
20. Gaza to Jerusalem (dir.)
21. Satiated
22. Genesis starter
24. Belief: comb. form
25. Jewish calendar
27. Sage Akiva
29. Pagan deities
32. Mount of Olives plenty
36. Prepares for *Pesach*
39. Seven (Hebrew)
40. Israeli city
41. Jacob's fifth

42. Bezalel study
44. *Treif* wiggler
45. Li'l __, Capp cartoon
47. Dancer with 61 Across
49. Monty Hall
51. Negev ship?
52. __ Bashevis Singer
54. Eilat, old style
58. Matriarchs
61. Dancer with 47 Across
62. Hebrew letter
64. Gad to Simeon
65. Asher's boy
67. Methuselah
69. *Macher* (English)
70. Killed biblically
71. Budge
72. Magic Carpet base
73. __ of David
74. Musician Getz
75. *Mishmash* (English)

Down

1. Jewish doughnut?
2. Service ender
3. TV comic Milt
4. *Nuns* (English)
5. Tardy
6. Son of Gad
7. That man
8. Joseph Hertz
9. NYC Jewish hub
10. Supply with Uzis
11. 1,003
12. Emulates Hoffman

13. Noah's boy
21. *The Nanny* star
23. Seder plate item
26. Kunstler organization
27. Eat (Yiddish)
28. Cheer
30. __Yoelson, Al Jolson
31. Bernstein to friends
33. *Vavs* (English)
34. First lady and namesakes
35. Transaction
36. Dressed

Puzzle 47

Across

1. Ha-Levi specialty
4. Acted the bigot
9. Uzis
13. Imitated Mauri Rose
14. Israeli wood
15. Seder plate item
16. Myra, pianist
17. Writer Gertrude
18. Naomi alias?
19. Exist
20. Mediterranean
21. Statue donned with Lazarus poem
23. *Das Kapital* author
26. Sixth day creation
27. Lauder
28. Title for Montefiore
30. Leah's daughter
34. Tu B'Shevat need?
36. Patriarchs
38. Hobby for Paul Newman
39. El-Al posting
42. Got away

44. Prior to Christians
46. Hebrew letter
47. Bugsy Siegel's club
49. Winger to friends
51. Afula to Degania (dir.)
53. Jewish mother's talent?
55. Scream
57. Levi Strauss specialty
61. Bezalel artwork
63. Sodom sister city
65. House for Rothschild
69. Speak
70. Dershowitz organization
71. Gershwin and Morris
72. Torah commentator
74. Son of Gad
75. Jacob after the angel
76. Acted the first son
77. Sharansky to friends
78. Ribicoff and Vigoda
79. *Peyes*
80. Last degree

Down

1. Plays for Sills
2. Sinai
3. Cantor and Goldman
4. First of the minor prophets
5. Bimahs
6. Gelilah act
7. *Fear No __*, Sharansky work
8. Levi Strauss material
9. Ancient Asian country
10. Sound from Daniel's den

11. Comedian Sahl
12. Remain
13. Lulav action
20. Angel's sign
22. Haman or Amalek
24. Scholar Baeck
25. Tribes
29. Eve starter
31. *Meshuggeneh* (English)
32. Enjoyed manna

33. Chammat Gader springs
35. Boxer Kaplan
37. __ Man, Doron Sheffer
39. Roasted on *Pesach*
40. Zeta Beta ___, fraternity
41. __ *Maamin*, Wiesel work
43. *Daled* (English)
45. *Simcha*
48. Wedding casualties
50. *Schnoor* (English)
52. Ever to Bialik
54. Three: comb. form
56. *Mashgiach* approved
58. Noah's landing pad
59. Victim of Ahab
60. Oasis offering
62. Rebel against Moses
64. Zilpah and Bilhah
65. __ 18, Uris novel
66. Ishmael progeny
67. *Hashem* (English)
68. Resnik's organization
73. Mt. Hermon activity
74. Columnist Landers

Puzzle 48

Across

1. Prayer for dew
4. Business degree
7. David O. Selznick
10. Ein gedi
13. Alias
14. Generation (Hebrew)
15. Gaza to Jerusalem (dir.)
16. Arkin and Jolson
17. Offering
18. 21
19. Golden Girl Arthur
20. Admirer
21. Ambassador Eban
23. Belief: comb. form
25. *Bonanza* dad
27. Western Wall tunnel
30. Seder
31. Haman's end
32. She saved Judah's line
34. Pursue
36. Held an Uzi
37. Air organization
40. Stooge Larry
41. Non-Hebrew tribe

42. *Mezuzah* touch
43. Imitate the "four sons"?
44. Peters specialty
45. Mother of Isaac
46. Cut
47. *Mitla* ___, Uris novel
48. Avram's wife
51. Day school namesake
55. Torah tops?
57. Owns
58. Competent
59. El-Al posting
60. Sound of awe
62. *Shluf* (English)
64. *Shikker*'s choice?
65. 100 agarot
66. __ *Maamin*, Wiesel work
67. 601
68. Emcee Caesar
69. Hebrew letter
70. Goldwyn company
71. Her
72. Eat (Yiddish)

Down

1. Desert station
2. Eilat gulf
3. Seder item
4. 1,510
5. Dangerous Dana's profession
6. Make *aliyah*
7. Winger to friends
8. ___ *Shabbat*

9. Via Maris
10. Israeli city
11. El-Al craft
12. *Lou Grant* actor
22. Dangerfield's hope
24. Sarah, Rachel, Leah, or Rebecca
26. Sid Gordon's stat.
28. *Shema* ender

29. Items on Schindler's list
33. Ten make a *minyan*
34. Finance degree
35. ___ *tadrut*
36. Golda Meir or Meyerson
37. Greenberg's position
38. Yoelson
39. Sacrifice residue
41. Exist
42. Buckwheat groats
44. David's wandering wife?
45. Pouch

46. Prophesized
47. Passover
48. *Havdalah* spices
49. Bandleader Shaw
50. Prepare the Seder bone
52. Sign of a Cohen
53. Island entry
54. Moses' camouflage
56. *Chad Gadya*
61. That man
63. Soupy's ammo

Puzzle 49

Across

1. ___ Mitzvah
4. *Treif* meat
7. Isaac stand-in
10. *Shluf* (English)
13. El-Al posting
14. Son of Gad
15. In front of
16. Stone or Bronze
17. Oral vaccine inventor
20. Streimel
21. Kamen or Freidman
22. Like *shiva* clothes
23. Perfect
24. Break the eighth
26. Brooks
27. She saved Judah's line
28. Cass Elliott
30. Comic Mort
32. *Feh*
35. Column
37. Etrog cousins
41. *Exodus* author Uris
43. Lulav action
45. Dropped
46. Plotting Persian guard
48. Ancestry
50. __ *Largo*, Bacall film
51. Danny DeVito's wife
53. Found in *charoset*
55. *Naches* (English)
58. Haman or Amalek
60. Elected
64. *Yeladim* (English)
65. Like Moses' bush
67. Talmud, __ Law
68. Before
69. The Kotel (2 words)
71. Archaeological mound
72. *Shikker*'s choice
73. Prophesize
74. "Thou" to Marceau
75. Goldman and Koch
76. Babi ___ , Ukraine
77. Prepare for Seder
78. *Nuns* (English)

Down

1. Moses' rays?
2. Israeli city
3. Seder locale
4. That one
5. Shaw and Shamsky
6. *Mess* (Yiddish)
7. Maccabees
8. Sinai climate
9. Ten make a *minyan*
10. Seventh minor prophet
11. 100th of an NIS
12. Actor Sellers
18. Village of Simeon
19. Exist
23. Fronds for Lulavs
25. Round for Spitz
27. __ *Seance* by Singer
29. Shertok or Feinstein
31. Service ender
32. Supreme (abbr.)

33. *Gimmel* (English)
34. Aaron's resting place
36. Prayer for dew
38. Tu B' Shevat planting
39. Be'ersheba to Jerusalem
    (dir.)
40. Arkia milieu
42. *Nebbishes*
44. *Tzedakah*
47. Her
49. And others (abbr.)
52. Nazi at times
54. Sid Caesar's __ *of Shows*
55. Center of the Seder
56. Ranted
57. Never in the temple!
59. Bezalel study
61. Emulate Abba Eban
62. Sasson's milieu
63. Island entry
65. Abzug
66. Life or Knowledge
69. Manner
70. Biblical fishing device

1	2	3		4	5	6		7	8	9		10	11	12
13				14				15				16		
17			18				19					20		
21					22						23			
24				25		26				27				
			28		29			30	31					
32	33	34		35			36		37			38	39	40
41			42		43			44			45			
46				47			48			49		50		
			51			52		53			54			
55	56	57				58	59			60		61	62	63
64					65				66		67			
68				69						70				
71				72				73				74		
75				76				77				78		

Puzzle 50

Across

1. Noah's boy
4. Seder bread
9. De Mille specialty
14. Alias
15. *Never__*, Kahane book
16. Defense minister Moshe
17. Marx brothers specialty
18. Papa Cartwright
20. Obey
22. Divorce paper
23. Maccabiah game
24. Haifa to Hebron (dir.)
27. Aaron's sister
32. Used a *mikveh*
35. Kol__
36. Mother (Hebrew)
39. Ammonite king
41. Mitzvah, good __
42. It is, to Bialik
43. Prior NYC mayor
44. Her
46. __ *carte*
47. Forty day forecast
49. Actor/Director Rob
51. Emcee Caesar
52. Rainbows
54. Stone or Segaloff
56. Source of balm
58. Literary initials
59. Israeli newspaper
63. Like Goliath
65. Join
66. Synagogues
73. __ *Promise*, by Potok
74. Dead Sea cosmetics
75. Sounds the Shofar
76. Emulated Moses
77. Hosea and Haggai
78. Sage Akiva
79. Arkin and Jolson

Down

1. Ishmael's mom
2. Gulf of __
3. Houdini's act
4. *Bris* must
5. Before
6. Sailor
7. Wilderness of __
8. ___ *Shabbat*
9. Philosopher Buber
10. Solomon's find
11. *Vav* (English)
12. King David?
13. Acre to Tiberias (dir.)
19. Netanya specialty
21. Winger to friends
24. Step
25. Uses his lulav
26. Wiggling *treif* fish
28. Got away
29. Einstein specialties
30. Son of Gad
31. Prophesizing elder
33. Fortas, casually
34. Eisner's organization
36. Lulav companion
37. Where Bubbe went?

38. Ezra's swift scribe
40. Seven (Hebrew)
45. In front of
48. Jerusalem to Tiberias (dir.)
50. __ a boy!
53. Cacti
55. Not: comb. form
57. Daniel's test site
60. "__Pass" (Uris)
61. Merman

62. Moses' camouflage
64. *Welcome Back Kotter* star
65. Refuseniks' homeland
66. Torah breastplate
67. Got ya!
68. *Tallit* holder
69. Eden dweller
70. 151
71. Register
72. Gives a shank

1	2	3		4	5	6	7	8		9	10	11	12	13
14				15						16				
17				18					19					
20			21					22						
23					24	25	26		27		28	29	30	31
			32	33				34		35				
36	37	38		39					40		41			
42				43				44		45		46		
47			48		49		50					51		
52				53		54					55			
56					57		58				59	60	61	62
				63		64				65				
66	67	68	69				70	71	72			73		
74					75							76		
77					78							79		

Puzzle 51

Across

1. Israeli mesa?
7. Make the *matzah*
11. *Shmatah* (English)
14. Says Kol Nidre
15. Actress Perlman
16. Art Shamsky stat.
17. "Where the Wild Things Are" illustrator
18. Paddles
19. *Gelilah* act
20. Meadow
22. *Schmutz* (English)
24. Baal __ Tov
28. Meir Kahane
31. Esther's kingdom?
32. The King David
34. Exist
35. __ *Hall*, Allen film
36. Noah's landing pad
38. Israeli wood
40. Goldwyn to friends
41. Writer Malamud
43. Betty Friedan's organization
46. Gabriel and Uriel headgear
47. Seder segment
49. Made *aliyah*
52. Guitarist Dylan
54. Seder locale
55. Cleo killers
56. Levi Strauss material
58. Calendar guide
59. Singer novel
61. *Potch* (English)
63. Aaron's co-leader
64. *Erevs* (English)
67. Like the ten tribes
72. ___ Mitzvah
73. Sabbath light
74. Elijah disciple
75. Sighs
76. Say the Viddui
77. Judah to Esau

Down

1. Matriarchs
2. Enjoyed *latkes*
3. Zimram to Abraham
4. *I __ Thou*, Martin Buber
5. Monty Hall specialty
6. Requestor
7. Issachar to Levi
8. Got ya!
9. Olympian Strug
10. Seder manner
11. Law of ___
12. Haman's eighth
13. *Bonanza* dad
21. Travel club
23. Stooge Larry
24. Political party
25. Dance
26. Village of Simeon
27. "Sea" to Wiesel
29. *Death Wish* star
30. Razor exec, Schick
33. Jacob's father-in-law

35. Israeli city
37. __ Aviv
39. Anger
42. Many-colored
43. Moses' last mount
44. Principles signing city
45. "If not now, _?", Hillel
46. Myra, pianist
48. Dike
49. Scholar Rabbi Adret
50. Son of Asher
51. Cosell's coverage

53. *Bissel* (English)
56. Old Israeli newspaper
57. Expert
60. *Tzedakah*
62. "__ of Settlement"
65. Mother (Hebrew)
66. Moe Berg
68. *Shikker*'s sip
69. Sort of? (ending)
70. Her
71. *Hee* __

Puzzle 52

Across

1. Village of Simeon
5. Tower
10. Actor/Director Reiner
13. Moses' last mount
14. Israeli city
15. Solomon's secret
16. Angel of Death path
17. Gaza __
18. Moses Ibn Ezra specialty
19. Saks or Macy's event
20. Oakland A's Holtzman
21. *Drek* (English)
22. Tsaban, Minister of immigration
24. Noah's messenger
26. Artist Ben
28. *Noshes* (English)
31. Research for Niels Bohr
32. Columnist Barrett
33. Li'l Abner creator
35. *Shikker*s
36. Baseball MVP
37. Piece for Tucker
38. Parker or Bialik
39. Ribicoff and Vigoda
40. Sage Akiva
41. UJA cards
43. The first son
44. Barney
45. Dershowitz bargain?
46. Sukkot
49. Male swan
50. Gangster "Dandy __"
54. Dance
55. Jonah's prison
57. Pierced as sign of bondsman
58. World (Hebrew)
59. "___ again": JDL motto
60. Hebrew letter
61. Koch and Land
62. Jacob and the Angel
63. __ year in Jerusalem!

Down

1. Son of Seth
2. Sandal maker
3. Cain's victim
4. *Dick Van Dyke Show* comedian
5. Artist Leonard
6. Later
7. *Chametz* before Pesach
8. Ithamar high priest
9. Round for Spitz
10. Not on *Shabbat*
11. ___ *Shabbat*
12. Miss America __ Meyerson
15. Reconstructionist
21. Hadassah employees
23. Expressions of ease
24. Roasted on *Pesach*
25. Esther's kingdom?
26. Crouch
27. The King David
28. Exodus leader
29. *Zaftig* (English)

30. Rosenberg or Caleb
31. Egyptian snake
32. Biblical garb
34. Herman Barron's score
36. *Shamatahs* (English)
40. Acre to Tiberias (dir.)
42. David O. Selznick
43. Einstein
45. *Chupah* holders

46. Teva offering
47. Grasp
48. Roman and Messianic
49. *Machpelah*
51. Amy Alcott target
52. Shofar source?
53. Etrog hand?
55. Jericho to Tel Aviv (dir.)
56. That one

Solutions

Puzzle 1

P	I	T	A	■	A	R	B	A	H	■	N	E	B	O
O	D	E	S	■	G	I	L	D	A	■	E	L	A	M
L	E	A	H	■	A	D	O	L	F	■	L	A	K	E
L	A	M	E	■	D	E	W	■	T	E	L	L	E	R
■	R	E	A	R	■	B	O	D	Y	■	■	■	■	■
P	E	R	I	S	H	■	B	O	R	E	■	S	S	E
O	R	A	T	E	■	G	R	O	A	N	■	C	I	A
L	I	C	E	■	C	L	O	T	H	■	M	O	E	S
I	C	E	■	E	L	A	T	H	■	B	O	R	G	E
O	H	S	■	B	A	T	H	■	P	R	U	N	E	D
■	C	A	R	T	■	T	E	A	R	■	■	■	■	■
A	R	M	O	N	I	■	Y	E	T	■	N	E	C	K
B	O	A	R	■	N	A	I	V	E	■	I	V	A	N
E	M	M	A	■	E	L	D	E	R	■	N	I	N	E
S	E	A	L	■	T	E	S	T	S	■	G	L	E	E

Puzzle 2

G	E	T	■	L	A	D	■	T	E	E	■	J	O	B
E	R	E	■	U	J	A	■	S	A	M	■	A	D	E
M	A	L	A	C	H	I	■	A	T	E	■	P	E	N
■	A	R	K	■	R	E	B	E	K	A	H	■	■	■
F	I	V	E	■	D	Y	L	A	N	■	R	E	A	D
E	R	I	■	H	A	M	A	N	■	M	I	T	L	A
H	A	V	D	A	L	A	H	■	M	A	S	H	E	D
■	E	D	E	N	■	M	A	M	A	■	■	■	■	■
M	O	S	S	A	D	■	M	A	R	R	I	A	G	E
A	R	M	E	D	■	D	A	N	C	E	■	R	A	Y
R	E	A	R	■	B	E	K	A	H	■	M	A	L	E
■	S	T	R	I	P	E	S	■	L	A	B	■	■	■
O	O	H	■	O	R	T	■	S	U	I	C	I	D	E
E	N	E	■	N	T	H	■	E	S	E	■	A	C	E
R	E	D	■	A	H	S	■	H	A	S	■	N	I	L

Puzzle 3

Puzzle 4

Puzzle 5

R	I	S	E	■	A	H	A	B	■	W	I	S	E
E	S	T	E	E	■	P	A	U	L	■	A	D	E	N
S	H	O	R	N	■	P	I	T	A	B	R	E	A	D
O	U	R	■	E	S	E	■	O	D	E	■	A	L	S
R	A	M	■	M	E	A	L	■	E	T	H	■		
T	H	Y	■	I	S	L	E	S	■	H	A	T	E	D
■	B	E	A	■	O	A	K	■	S	O	R	E		
M	O	S	E	S	M	O	N	T	E	F	I	O	R	E
O	N	E	G	■	E	R	A	■	D	I	D	■		
B	E	G	A	N	■	T	R	E	E	S	■	D	A	D
■	T	E	T	■	D	I	S	H	■	A	R	E		
T	H	E	■	B	A	T	■	S	H	E	■	N	I	S
H	A	S	M	O	N	E	A	N	■	R	A	I	S	E
E	T	A	M	■	G	A	B	E	■	S	H	E	A	R
E	H	U	D	■	O	M	E	R	■	S	L	I	T	

Puzzle 6

E	D	S	■	Z	I	M	■	M	C	C	■	M	A	D
F	E	E	■	A	C	E	■	I	R	A	■	E	R	A
F	E	L	A	F	E	L	■	D	I	P	■	R	A	N
S	P	L	I	T	■	S	P	I	E	S	■	A	B	C
■	R	I	B	■	H	A	D	■	B	R	I	E		
A	W	L	■	G	O	L	A	N	■	A	L	I	A	S
A	H	A	B	■	O	U	R	■	S	Y	A	■		
R	O	B	E	R	T	Z	I	M	M	E	R	M	A	N
■	N	I	S	■	S	E	A	■	E	A	S	T		
S	P	E	N	D	■	B	E	L	L	S	■	R	A	H
H	A	L	O	■	J	O	E	■	L	I	E	■		
E	R	E	■	C	U	R	S	E	■	D	R	E	S	S
V	A	V	■	A	D	D	■	M	A	N	I	L	O	W
A	D	E	■	V	E	E	■	E	W	E	■	A	N	A
T	E	N	■	E	A	R	■	K	E	Y	■	M	G	M

Puzzle 7

```
O A K   A G A M     D E A T H
R B I   G A M E   H A G G A I
T A S   A L A S   A N G E L S
    H A I L   S P I N S
S H O R N   B A R R Y   B A S
H U N T   S A G E S   B E N S
E R R   M O S E S   A R T I E
    I N A N E   E I L A T
M A V E N   B A N D S   E T A
C H E T   S A L T S   O M E R
C A R   H I L L S   S W I N E
    L A D L E   M I N D
D E S I R E   N E I L   L O T
A L T A R S   B A L L   E N E
D I A R Y   Y U K S   R E D
```

Puzzle 8

```
D O T   S S E   S S W     I S M
C O W   T A S   A W E   S T A
C H O L E N T   F O E   R A N
    B E R G   H E R   S A L T
A R Y A N   N O T E   H E L L
D O T H   H O L Y   F A L S E
L A W   B A A L   M A N
    D O R O T H Y P A R K E R
    H A H   W A R M   L I P
S A T Y R   P O L E   B E T A
A D A M   S H O E   L E P E R
M A L E   H I D   B O T H
E L L   A I L   M I C H A E L
C I I   A N I   A R K   N N E
H A T   A S P   C D S   T E N
```

Puzzle 9

```
U J A · H A T · · S P Y · M C C
S K I · O D E · · I I I · A A A
A L R O S E N · S A D · I N N
· · P I T S · P E N · C L A D
B E L L S · H E R O · H E A L
A L A S · P I T A · L O R N E
H I N · W I D E · T A S · ·
· M E D I T E R R A N E A N ·
· · A N Y · F O L D · F A N
S H A R E · S A L E · F I S T
W A N T · B I L L · P E K A H
E G G S · A R K · S O L O ·
A G E · R U E · C H E L M N O
T A L · B E N · D A M · A N N
S I S · I R S · E S S · N E E
```

Puzzle 10

```
G A G · E T A · P A W · C A P
I C E · A W L · A T E · A H A
G E N E S I S · R O E · M A R
· · O X E N · C A N · H E R S
C E C I L · B A D E · E L A H
O B I T · G A T E · K A S H A
D A D · O A R S · C I V · ·
· L E T S M A K E A D E A L ·
· · A L E · I R A S · S E E
M A M B O · C L A N · S H A S
O R A L · M E L S · D E E D S
R I D E · O N S · F E A R ·
I S M · E S T · O R A L L A W
A A A · S H E · W E T · E L I
H I N · E E R · N T H · V A T
```

Puzzle 11

S	H	E	■	S	T	A	B	L	E	■	O	M	E	N
H	A	L	■	I	S	R	A	E	L	■	R	O	S	E
E	M	A	■	R	A	M	B	A	M	■	G	R	E	W
B	A	T	H	■	D	E	E	■	■	Y	A	D	.	■
A	S	H	A	M	E	D	■	P	L	A	N	E	S	■
■	■	I	B	S	■	■	B	E	E	R	■	C	A	L
S	A	B	R	A	■	N	A	T	A	N	■	H	B	O
O	B	E	Y	■	R	I	S	E	N	■	V	A	I	N
U	R	N	■	H	O	M	E	R	■	B	E	I	N	G
R	A	G	■	E	N	O	S	■	T	R	I	■	■	■
■	M	U	R	R	A	Y	■	W	E	A	L	T	H	Y
■	■	R	I	B	■	■	A	R	M	■	S	H	O	E
R	A	I	N	■	A	L	C	A	P	P	■	I	N	N
A	M	O	S	■	S	E	T	T	L	E	■	N	O	T
M	I	N	E	■	H	O	S	H	E	A	■	E	R	A

Puzzle 12

B	A	K	E	■	B	A	A	L	S	■	L	J	C
E	R	A	S	■	A	L	C	O	T	T	■	A	A	A
F	A	D	E	■	B	I	T	T	E	R	■	G	I	N
O	R	E	■	H	E	Y	■	■	P	E	B	B	L	E
R	A	S	H	I	■	A	B	E	■	F	R	O	■	■
E	T	H	E	L	■	H	A	L	O	■	O	M	R	I
■	■	A	L	S	■	H	A	R	P	■	E	B	B	
J	E	Z	R	E	E	L	■	H	A	L	P	R	I	N
A	N	I	■	L	I	E	S	■	L	E	E	■	■	
W	E	P	T	■	R	A	Y	S	■	A	R	B	A	H
■	P	A	N	■	F	A	A	■	S	T	O	L	E	
S	H	O	F	A	R	■	T	E	E	■	N	I	L	
O	U	R	■	M	A	A	R	I	V	■	A	N	E	M
R	N	A	■	E	M	P	I	R	E	■	P	I	N	E
E	T	H	■	S	E	D	E	R	■	T	E	S	T	

Puzzle 13

B	A	B	I		C	A	S	S		A	H	A	Z	
A	L	A	S		O	T	T	O		L	I	K	U	D
N	A	S	A		N	E	I	L	S	E	D	A	K	A
K	N	E	A	D			L	E	E			B	O	Y
		C	O	R	A	L		A	L	T	A	R	S	
A	S	H		S	U	R	E		T	I	E			
S	H	O	W		T	Y	R	E		K	A	S	H	A
P	O	R	A	T	H	A		S	H	E	C	H	E	M
S	T	A	I	R		N	A	T	E		H	I	R	E
		L	E	D		S	E	A	L		N	O	N	
D	E	M	S	K	Y		P	E	R	E	S			
A	L	A			A	S	A			N	E	E	D	S
S	I	M	E	O	N	I	T	E	S		E	L	A	H
H	A	M	A	N		T	H	E	E		R	I	T	E
	M	A	T	E		S	A	L	E		S	E	E	M

Puzzle 14

	S	L	I	P		S	T	A	N		M	O	T	O
S	H	A	R	E		H	O	B	O		E	L	A	M
L	A	B	A	N		A	R	I	D		L	A	K	E
I	D	O	L		S	W	A	M		H	O	M	E	R
T	E	R	E	S	H		H	E	R	O	D			
		V	E	E			L	A	W	Y	E	R	S	
J	A	M	I	E		P	I	E	C	E		B	I	O
O	M	E	N		D	A	N	C	E		F	A	S	T
E	M	S		B	E	L	C	H		P	O	L	E	S
Y	O	S	S	E	L	E		D	O	R				
	W	E	I	S	S		O	P	E	R	A	S		
Z	O	H	A	R		T	O	P	S		H	A	L	O
E	V	E	R		W	I	N	O		W	E	I	L	L
T	E	A	M		E	N	G	R		E	A	S	E	D
A	R	T	S		T	E	S	T		E	D	E	N	

Puzzle 15

	R	O	B	E		B	R	I	S		M	E	N	U
B	E	L	L	S		N	I	B	S		O	V	E	R
E	D	D	I	E		A	N	N	E		M	I	I	I
A	D	E	N		B	I	G		W	E	L	L	S	
M	Y	R	T	L	E		S	A	B	I	N			
		Z	I	N	G		B	A	T	T	L	E	S	
E	S	T	E	E		E	A	R	T	H		A	L	A
A	L	A	S		A	R	I	A	S		S	W	I	M
S	I	X		P	S	A	L	M		M	O	S	E	S
E	P	I	T	A	P	H		S	E	E	D			
		S	I	S	S	Y		S	T	O	O	G	E	
H	A	M	A	N		E	M	S		M	A	R	A	
A	R	I	D		T	O	N	E		W	I	S	E	R
L	A	K	E		A	R	T	S		S	T	I	E	S
O	D	E	S		S	E	A	S		W	E	S	T	

Puzzle 16

	S	E	E	D		R	A	C	E		H	A	L	F
A	H	A	V	A		O	L	A	M		O	R	A	L
R	I	T	E	S		S	I	N	S		L	I	M	E
O	V	E	N		B	E	E	T		A	I	D	E	D
D	A	N	I	T	E		N	I	D	R	E			
		N	I	T			C	I	T	R	O	N	S	
F	R	O	G	S		M	A	L	E	S		D	O	T
R	I	B	S		M	O	S	E	S		B	E	T	A
U	S	E		F	O	R	K	S		W	I	S	E	R
M	E	D	D	L	E	D		D	O	G			
		O	A	S	E	S		L	E	T	T	E	R	
S	T	R	U	G		C	H	A	I		H	A	L	O
A	R	A	B		A	H	A	B		B	A	B	E	S
N	E	I	L		S	A	L	E		E	N	O	C	H
G	E	N	E		H	I	L	L		D	A	R	T	

Puzzle 17

I	R	K		T	A	F		F	A	Y		S	E	T
D	N	A		E	R	E		A	L	A		E	L	I
S	A	B	B	A	T	H		M	E	R		S	E	G
	B	A	R	S		H	I	P		H	A	V	E	
C	L	A	N	S		M	A	S	H		O	M	E	R
C	O	L	D		D	A	S	H		O	M	E	N	S
C	F	A		N	O	R	M		A	B	E			
	T	H	R	E	E	C	O	R	N	E	R	E	D	
	E	R	R		N	E	E	D		D	I	E		
S	H	R	E	D		S	E	A	M		B	O	N	E
H	E	E	D		G	L	A	D		G	I	M	E	L
E	L	M	S		R	A	N		B	A	B	I		
B	E	E		L	I	V		S	E	M	I	T	E	S
A	N	D		E	N	E		A	L	E		E	R	A
H	A	Y		A	D	S		T	A	S		S	I	X

Puzzle 18

B	U	M		H	A	L		F	E	H		T	A	S
E	L	I		E	R	I		A	Z	A		H	B	O
A	P	T		Y	A	K		A	R	M		E	N	D
M	A	L	L		D	U	B		A	M	A	D	E	O
S	N	A	I	L		D	A	B		A	L	A	R	M
	P	E	A	K		B	E	T	T	E				
A	L	A		T	E	K	I	A	H		P	A	L	E
W	E	S	T	E	R	N		R	I	C	H	L	E	R
E	A	S	E		R	E	A	D	E	R		B	E	A
	A	S	I	E	L		F	I	N	E				
E	L	E	C	T		L	A	B		B	I	R	D	S
D	I	S	H	E	S		N	O	W		S	T	A	N
G	O	T		P	O	P		A	R	T		S	Y	A
E	N	E		U	R	I		R	A	H		O	A	K
S	S	E		P	E	N		S	P	Y		N	N	E

Puzzle 19

S	A	M	E				T	H	R	O	W			T	E	T
T	R	A	S	H			S	I	N	A	I			H	O	R
R	I	N	S	E		A	D	A	R	S	H	E	N	I		
A	D	D			Y	A	D			S	E	A	S			
P	A	L	M		B	E	R	G		R	I	T	E	S		
S	I	N	G	E	R		O	U	R		R	I	D	E		
		M	B	A		B	L	O	W		N	N	E			
A	D	S		A	H	A		F	B	I		G	A	D		
B	A	H		L	A	N	D		E	N	E					
E	V	E	S		M	E	L		R	E	D	S	E	A		
L	E	P	E	R		M	I	S	T		S	E	L	L		
		H	E	A	T		H	A	Y			S	E	T		
B	E	E	R	S	H	E	B	A		A	H	A	V	A		
A	A	R		H	E	R	O	D		H	O	M	E	R		
Y	U	D		I	M	A	G	E			T	E	N	S		

Puzzle 20

A	L	S		L	F	H		L	E	E		H	A	M
R	O	T		A	R	E		I	B	S		A	G	O
B	R	A	I	D	E	D		B	A	S	E	M	A	N
A	R	I	D		T	O	K	E	N		D	A	R	T
H	E	R	O	D		N	I	L		I	M	N	A	H
		L	E	W	I	S		T	O	O				
A	R	M		B	E	S	S		A	U	N	T	I	E
B	A	B	E		E	M	I	M	S		D	E	N	S
A	M	A	L	E	K		N	A	T	E		N	N	E
		D	R	S		G	R	E	A	T				
K	E	T	E	R		E	E	R		T	R	A	S	H
A	P	E	S		M	A	R	A	H		A	R	I	A
S	H	A	T	N	E	R		N	E	W	P	O	R	T
H	O	R		O	I	L		O	R	E		S	E	E
A	D	S		D	R	Y		S	S	E		E	N	D

Puzzle 21

```
E F F . . S H E . B E G . H A T
L I I . . S E T . E R A . E G O
L E N . . E R R . T E L . L A W
I R A S . M O B . V I O L I N .
S Y N A G O G U E . L I O N S .
. C L A N . C A M E L . . . . .
F R I E D . T H R E E . B E E .
A B E S . D E A L T . O A K S .
A I R . B I A L Y . G A T E S .
. E L E C T . B U S H . . . . .
A G A R A . H E D O N I S T S .
K A D E S H . R U N . S H O E .
A D L . T O P . N N E . E V E .
B Y E . E M A . A I L . B A R .
A A R . D E N . M E L . A H S .
```

Puzzle 22

```
. N E B O . E M M A . T A L E .
E A T E N . Y A E L . Y E A R .
L O R N E . E Z R A . R O N A .
A M O S . U S E . B A N D S . .
L I G H T S . L A B A N . . . .
. A H A Z . R E S T I N G . . .
B A T H E . E S T E E . R O E .
E B A N . B R A I N . M A S T .
E L L . N E E D S . B O N E S .
S E L L E R S . T E A R . . . .
. E I G H T . A N T H E M . . .
S E G A L . H A T . S O L O . .
A R A D . S T A R . M A S K S .
M U T E . T A N K . C H E A T .
E V E R . Y U K S . C L A N . .
```

Puzzle 23

F	I	N	■	C	A	R	■	S	S	W	■	G	A	L
A	B	A	■	U	R	I	■	A	M	A	■	I	R	E
D	E	S	E	R	T	S	■	T	A	S	■	L	A	M
E	X	A	L	T	■	E	R	I	C	H	■	B	R	O
■	■	L	I	E	■	I	R	K	■	J	O	A	N	
E	M	A	■	S	I	E	G	E	■	G	O	A	T	S
G	A	Z	A	■	L	F	H	■	E	E	K	■	■	
G	R	A	C	E	A	F	T	E	R	M	E	A	L	S
■	H	I	T	■	E	E	R	■	R	H	E	A		
B	A	L	A	K	■	C	O	L	O	R	■	A	D	D
A	D	E	N	■	E	A	U	■	R	E	D	■		
L	A	P	■	B	L	E	S	S	■	F	I	R	S	T
A	L	E	■	A	D	S	■	E	D	O	M	I	T	E
A	I	R	■	B	E	A	■	N	O	R	■	D	A	N
M	A	S	■	E	R	R	■	D	A	M	■	E	N	D

Puzzle 24

■	C	A	L	F	■	S	W	I	N	G	■	Y	A	P
P	A	P	E	R	■	M	A	R	O	R	■	A	L	E
E	M	P	T	Y	■	O	R	A	T	E	■	E	T	A
L	E	E	■	E	A	T	■	E	A	G	L	E	■	
T	R	A	P	■	B	E	A	M	■	T	E	A	R	S
S	A	L	A	M	I	■	S	E	A	■	T	R	E	E
■	R	A	G	■	H	A	L	F	■	A	G	E		
H	A	M	■	L	A	B	■	T	E	L	■	D	O	R
E	S	T	■	L	I	A	R	■	F	E	H	■		
S	H	A	S	■	L	E	N	■	B	E	A	S	T	S
S	E	R	A	H	■	R	A	C	E	■	T	H	E	E
■	R	A	M	A	H	■	A	T	E	■	A	R	E	
S	I	R	■	R	O	Y	A	L	■	L	I	K	U	D
S	T	A	■	A	R	I	S	E	■	I	D	E	A	S
W	E	T	■	N	A	D	A	B	■	M	A	S	H	

Puzzle 25

A	W	E		H	E	M		C	I	A		W	A	R
R	I	D		A	L	E		A	S	A		E	L	I
A	D	D		S	A	M	U	E	L	R	U	B	I	N
B	O	I	L		H	O	R	S	E		S	E	A	S
S	W	E	A	T		R	N	A		C	U	R	S	E
		B	A	B	I		R	E	A	R				
E	L	M		F	L	A	G		S	P	E	A	R	S
B	E	A	T		E	L	E	C	T		R	I	B	S
B	O	X	E	R	S		T	H	E	M		L	I	E
		R	O	S	H		A	E	O	N				
D	A	L	E	D		A	H	S		B	A	T	H	S
E	G	O	S		S	N	A	I	L		P	O	E	M
N	A	C	H	M	A	N	I	D	E	S		U	R	I
I	R	K		A	L	A		I	N	K		R	O	T
M	A	S		N	T	H		M	D	I		O	D	E

Puzzle 26

S	I	L	L	S		E	R	R		M	E	T	S	
A	S	I	E	L		A	A	A		C	R	I	E	S
T	H	E	V	I	C	T	I	M		C	A	T	C	H
		I	D	A		D	A	B		S	H	O	E	
T	W	O		E	L	L		H	A	T		E	N	D
H	E	A	D		F	A	B		B	E	A	R	D	S
E	S	T	E	E		B	E	H	I	N	D			
E	T	H	E	L		A	G	O		T	A	B	O	R
		P	L	A	N	E	S		S	M	O	T	E	
Y	A	S	S	I	R		T	E	L		S	I	T	S
E	R	E		S	I	D		A	I	R		L	O	T
N	A	S	A		D	A	D		C	I	A			
T	R	A	D	E		N	E	T	E	N	Y	A	H	U
L	A	M	E	D		C	A	R		S	A	L	E	S
	T	E	N	S		E	L	I		E	N	E	M	Y

Puzzle 27

E	L	I		M	E	R		M	B	A		R	B	I
N	I	S		A	L	A		A	A	R		O	U	R
E	P	H	R	A	I	M		A	C	A	D	A	M	E
		M	A	M	M	A		R	O	B	E	S		
M	I	A	M	I		T	W	I	N		S	T	A	R
O	D	E		N	E	G	E	V		N	E	E	D	Y
B	A	L	M		Y	A	D		G	I	R	D	L	E
		O	M	E	N		S	A	L	T				
M	A	M	B	O	S		G	E	M		S	O	L	D
A	R	I	S	E		L	E	P	E	R		B	A	R
R	E	N	T		S	E	T	H		A	D	A	M	S
	Y	E	N	T	A		A	R	M	E	D			
S	E	A	R	O	A	D		R	U	B	B	I	S	H
P	E	N		A	T	E		D	N	A		A	S	A
A	L	S		H	E	R		I	S	M		H	E	M

Puzzle 28

A	L	E	F		M	A	S	O	N		G	E	N	E
K	A	Y	E		I	M	A	G	E		U	R	I	M
A	B	E	L		N	I	D	R	E		M	I	L	A
		F	L	O	O	D		E	D	O	M			
A	G	O		A	R	A	B		H	O	S	E	A	
H	E	R	B	S		H	A	M	A	S		I	L	L
A	M	A	L	E	K		T	A	L		E	M	M	A
	N	O	S	E	S		C	A	R	D	O			
B	L	E	W		E	S	T		S	I	N	N	E	D
R	A	Y		S	P	E	A	K		D	A	D	D	A
O	P	E	R	A		F	A	D	E		U	S	Y	
		O	M	E	R		H	O	R	E	B			
V	I	S	A		L	U	L	A	V		A	N	N	E
E	R	A	S		A	L	O	N	E		S	O	N	S
T	E	X	T		M	E	D	E	S		E	W	E	S

Puzzle 29

```
R A M   O B E D     F R A M E
U S E   M E R E   B R O K E N
N A Y   E L A L   R O M A N S
    E D N A   I M A G E
P E R E S   G L A S S   M C C
I S L E   B E A M S   I I I I
E T A   B A T H E   A R K I A
    N E E D S   L A T K E
J E S S E   M A U D E   W H O
L A K E   B A S K S   C A I N
C R Y   H O R S E   S A L T S
    B O O T Y   K A R L
D E S E R T   R A N G   A L E
A G U N A H   I D E A   C A N
B O N D S     A D E N   E W E
```

Puzzle 30

```
L A M E   S P L I T   C H A D
A R O D   A L O N E   R I D E
H I S S   M A N N A   I R A N
R A H   S U N G   C H E E R S
    E S T E E   S H A S
T S A H A L   C H E T   M U D
A A R O N   D O O R S   E N E
S L E W   C A V E S   M I I I
T E N   H O L E S   P O R T S
E M S   O V E R   B A S K E T
    B R E D   P A S T A
S U S A N N   L E G S   H O G
O R A L   A F I R E   S A M E
M I L A   N O V E L   A N E M
E M E K   T R E S S   Y E N S
```

Puzzle 31

Puzzle 32

Puzzle 33

G	I	L	D	■	A	R	A	B	■	A	B	N	E	R
A	R	I	A	■	H	O	L	E	■	B	E	N	N	O
G	A	L	L	■	A	C	R	E	■	B	R	E	E	D
■	L	E	E	■	K	O	R	M	A	N	■	■	■	■
A	M	I	D	A	H	■	S	I	R	■	S	I	D	E
I	D	A	■	R	A	C	E	■	S	I	T	C	O	M
R	I	N	G	■	L	O	N	G	■	S	E	E	R	S
■	■	O	S	L	O	■	L	E	H	I	■	■	■	■
B	E	R	L	E	■	L	I	E	D	■	N	A	S	A
A	G	A	D	A	H	■	S	E	E	D	■	B	O	Y
R	O	N	A	■	E	R	R	■	N	A	T	I	V	E
■	■	■	M	O	R	I	A	H	■	B	A	G	■	■
L	A	M	E	D	■	V	E	E	S	■	B	A	R	E
A	B	B	I	E	■	E	L	A	H	■	L	I	N	E
P	E	A	R	S	■	R	I	D	E	■	E	L	A	L

Puzzle 34

■	B	A	Y	■	R	A	B	B	I	■	G	A	M	E
H	O	R	A	■	A	L	I	A	S	■	E	B	A	N
A	R	I	D	■	S	I	D	R	A	■	N	E	R	D
I	D	S	■	S	H	E	■	R	A	M	E	S	E	S
F	E	A	S	T	I	N	G	■	C	A	R	■	■	■
A	R	I	S	E	■	S	A	T	■	C	A	C	T	I
■	■	E	A	R	■	B	R	A	■	L	O	A	N	■
E	E	R	■	L	E	D	■	I	B	S	■	N	U	N
S	T	A	N	■	D	A	Y	■	A	A	A	■	■	■
S	C	H	U	L	■	N	O	W	■	L	I	K	U	D
■	■	■	M	A	S	■	M	A	D	E	L	I	N	E
S	H	A	B	B	A	T	■	R	A	M	■	D	I	I
W	I	D	E	■	G	I	A	N	T	■	A	R	T	S
A	D	A	R	■	E	S	T	E	E	■	P	O	E	M
M	E	M	S	■	S	H	E	D	S	■	E	N	D	■

Puzzle 35

H	A	M			A	B	E	S				S	T	E	V	E
E	G	O			R	O	S	H			S	T	O	G	I	E
Y	O	U			O	T	T	O			H	A	N	G	A	R
		N	O	S	H		W	E	A	R	Y					
T	I	T	H	E			D	E	A	L	S			G	A	B
A	R	M	S			F	I	R	S	T			M	E	N	U
L	E	O			Y	E	A	S	T			B	E	N	N	Y
		R	E	A	D	S			W	H	A	L	E			
S	P	I	E	D			P	L	A	I	T			H	A	S
P	E	A	K			D	O	E	R	S			D	A	R	K
Y	A	H			H	E	R	O	D			C	A	C	T	I
			L	A	B	A	N			D	U	S	K			
D	E	S	E	R	T			A	D	A	R			M	E	N
A	L	T	A	R	S			R	I	T	E			A	M	I
D	I	A	R	Y			D	E	E	S			N	A	P	

Puzzle 36

A	H	S			D	O	T			M	E	M			O	F	T
B	E	T			A	M	A			A	L	A			S	I	R
R	A	A	M	S	E	S			M	I	R	A	C	L	E		
A	R	I	A			R	H	Y	M	E			M	A	M	A	
M	O	N	T	H			L	A	Y			F	I	R	S	T	
			H	A	S	I	D			B	E	D					
D	A	N			M	M	C	V			R	E	A	D	E	R	
A	L	E	F			A	H	A	V	A			H	O	R	A	
M	E	T	R	I	C			S	L	I	T			S	A	M	
			I	R	K			H	A	D	A	D					
I	S	L	E	S			F	E	D			L	A	M	E	D	
S	H	I	N			M	I	M	I	C			D	A	N	A	
C	A	N	D	L	E	S			M	I	S	S	I	O	N		
A	R	E			E	S	T			I	T	S			D	C	C
H	I	S			E	S	S			R	Y	E			S	H	E

Puzzle 37

```
.  M  O  S  T  .  D  R  A  N  K  .  A  M  A
S  A  R  A  H  .  A  B  D  O  N  .  M  A  D
T  S  A  D  E  .  N  I  D  R  E  .  M  R  S
A  C  T  .  E  T  C  .  .  M  A  Y  O  R  .
R  O  O  F  .  H  E  A  T  .  D  U  N  A  M
S  T  R  I  P  E  .  D  I  P  .  D  I  N  E
.  .  B  A  H  .  E  N  O  S  .  T  O  E  .
O  F  T  .  S  O  B  .  Y  E  A  .  E  S  T
P  A  R  .  S  P  E  D  .  T  U  B  .  .  .
E  L  U  L  .  E  A  U  .  E  L  I  J  A  H
N  A  M  E  S  .  T  O  Y  S  .  B  A  R  A
.  S  P  O  O  N  .  .  E  S  E  .  V  A  V
S  H  E  .  D  A  D  D  A  .  A  F  I  R  E
S  A  T  .  O  S  C  A  R  .  S  A  T  A  N
E  S  S  .  M  A  I  D  S  .  E  A  S  T  .
```

Puzzle 38

```
A  B  E  S  .  Y  A  D  S  .  D  E  A  L  S
H  A  L  T  .  E  L  A  H  .  A  T  L  I  T
A  D  A  R  .  T  E  V  A  .  S  H  E  B  A
Z  E  L  I  G  .  F  I  L  T  H  .  N  E  T
.  .  P  O  P  .  D  O  A  .  R  U  L  E  .
B  O  B  .  D  O  C  .  M  U  S  E  .  .  .
A  V  E  .  D  E  L  I  .  .  C  A  M  E  L
B  E  N  J  A  M  I  N  C  A  R  D  O  Z  O
E  N  D  O  R  .  .  C  A  R  O  .  A  R  T
.  .  A  D  A  M  .  N  I  L  .  B  A  S  .
K  A  H  N  .  T  A  S  .  A  L  S  .  .  .
A  L  E  .  F  E  V  E  R  .  S  T  A  F  F
S  T  A  I  R  .  E  G  O  S  .  E  B  A  L
H  A  R  R  Y  .  N  A  S  A  .  A  B  L  E
A  R  O  S  E  .  S  L  E  W  .  L  A  K  E
```

Puzzle 39

M	O	B	■	D	A	M	■	G	A	B	■	F	O	E
A	N	I	■	A	R	T	■	A	L	A	■	A	D	E
D	E	G	A	N	I	A	■	B	L	A	S	T	E	R
■	O	S	C	A	R	■	B	E	L	C	H	■	■	■
T	I	T	H	E	■	A	L	A	N	■	R	E	A	D
E	R	R	■	S	A	R	A	I	■	B	O	R	G	E
D	A	Y	S	■	D	A	D	■	J	O	L	S	O	N
■	■	C	O	A	T	■	B	O	W	L	■	■	■	■
M	O	T	H	E	R	■	W	A	S	■	S	P	I	N
E	R	R	O	R	■	B	A	U	E	R	■	R	B	I
M	E	A	L	■	B	U	R	T	■	O	M	E	N	S
■	C	A	S	A	S	■	I	S	L	E	S	■	■	■
C	H	E	R	I	S	H	■	S	E	L	L	E	R	S
C	A	R	■	D	E	E	■	T	E	E	■	N	A	P
C	D	S	■	E	S	S	■	A	D	D	■	T	H	Y

Puzzle 40

E	T	H	■	S	A	T	■	S	O	N	■	A	L	S
F	R	O	■	A	M	I	■	E	M	A	■	V	E	T
F	E	L	D	M	A	N	■	M	E	T	■	E	G	O
S	E	E	R	S	■	A	F	I	R	E	■	D	E	N
■	■	S	O	B	■	I	T	S	■	B	O	N	E	■
L	E	A	■	N	I	D	R	E	■	R	E	N	D	S
A	R	I	A	■	M	A	S	■	M	B	A	■	■	■
B	A	R	B	R	A	S	T	R	E	I	S	A	N	D
■	■	B	A	H	■	B	A	D	■	T	R	U	E	■
S	P	A	I	N	■	P	A	G	A	N	■	E	N	E
P	E	R	E	■	S	I	S	■	D	O	S	■	■	■
E	R	I	■	N	E	G	E	V	■	S	A	L	T	S
E	S	S	■	A	D	L	■	I	S	H	M	A	E	L
C	I	A	■	S	E	E	■	E	Y	E	■	W	E	E
H	A	I	■	A	R	T	■	W	A	R	■	S	S	W

Puzzle 41

O	T	T	O		A	D	A	R		H	A	M	A	N
S	O	U	R		B	A	R	A		A	G	A	R	A
C	U	R	E		E	R	E	V		M	E	R	O	M
A	R	K		A	S	K		E	M	A		C	D	E
R	O	S	E	N			I	N	A	N	E			
		S	T	E	P	S		S	T	E	V	E	N	
C	H	A	S	I	D	I	M		A	K	I	V	A	
H	A	M		S	S	E		D	A	S		L	I	I
A	T	O	N	E			W	I	N	C	H	E	L	L
D	E	N	I	M	S		A	V	I	H	U			
		L	I	A	R	S			E	M	C	E	E	
U	F	O		T	W	O		C	O	N		A	S	A
R	A	S	H	I		B	A	L	M		S	I	T	S
I	S	L	E	S		E	L	I	E		T	R	E	E
S	T	O	R	M		S	E	I	R		Y	O	E	L

Puzzle 42

P	L	A	Y		C	A	P	P		C	A	R	O
L	O	B	E	S		A	B	L	E		A	M	O	N
E	A	R	T	H		M	A	U	R	I	R	O	S	E
D	N	A		A	P	E		M	E	R		S	E	G
G	E	M		B	A	R	A		S	A	C			
E	D	S		B	R	A	T	S		S	H	E	M	A
		W	A	S		O	U	R		I	R	A	N	
J	O	N	A	T	H	A	N	P	O	L	L	A	R	D
A	D	E	N		A	L	E		M	A	D			
B	E	T	T	E		A	R	Y	A	N		D	A	D
		S	T	A		S	A	N	D		A	R	E	
C	F	A		A	D	L		S	S	E		N	I	S
H	A	N	D	M	A	I	D	S		R	A	I	S	E
E	D	N	A		M	M	I	I		S	H	E	A	R
T	E	E	S		S	E	E	R		S	L	I	T

Puzzle 43

B	I	G		P	L	O		T	A	S		S	I	R
A	D	E		A	I	R		A	B	C		H	B	O
B	E	N		R	A	G		F	E	H		A	Z	A
Y	A	E	L	A	R	A	D		S	A	B	R	A	S
	B	E	D		N	E	T		P	R	I	N	T	
L	O	A	V	E	S		A	R	K	I	A			
O	M	R	I		H	O	L	I	E	R		D	A	B
O	E	R		D	O	R		B	R	O		O	N	E
T	R	Y		R	O	A	M	E	R		G	U	N	S
	B	E	T	T	E		I	M	A	G	E	S		
O	A	S	E	S		E	R	A		E	T	H		
P	R	E	A	C	H		E	V	I	D	E	N	C	E
E	E	R		H	E	X		D	I	D		U	R	N
R	N	A		E	R	I		A	I	L		T	O	V
A	S	H		R	B	I		T	I	E		S	P	Y

Puzzle 44

S	A	M		A	L	A		W	S	W		Y	A	P
U	S	A		D	O	R		I	C	E		O	R	E
B	A	R	B	A	R	A		S	H	A	M	S	K	Y
	C	A	L	E	B		D	U	K	E	S			
B	E	E	R	I		I	D	O	L		N	E	E	D
E	R	A		A	L	A	R	M		V	A	L	O	R
D	R	U	M		A	N	Y		C	O	H	E	N	S
	T	O	P	S		H	O	W	E					
F	L	A	M	E	S		O	O	H		M	M	D	C
E	I	G	E	R		B	U	R	N	S		A	I	R
H	E	A	R		S	O	T	S		P	A	L	E	Y
	G	O	A	T	S		E	L	I	K	A			
S	H	I	N	B	E	T		M	I	R	A	C	L	E
S	I	T		B	R	O		A	M	I		H	A	M
E	N	E		A	N	N		N	E	T		I	D	A

Puzzle 45

A	B	A		N	N	E		T	A	S		R	A	G
S	U	N		T	O	P		E	R	A		A	G	O
H	I	T		H	A	H		D	A	B		N	N	W
E	L	I	E		H	O	G		D	R	A	G	O	N
S	T	O	R	M		D	A	S		A	R	E	N	S
		C	R	I	B		V	E	R	S	E			
I	S	H		S	I	S	E	R	A		L	Y	R	E
S	H	U	T	T	L	E		V	I	S	I	O	N	S
M	E	S	S		K	E	D	E	S	H		M	A	S
			A	B	O	D	E		E	A	S	T		
S	H	A	D	E		S	A	D		W	E	E	K	S
H	O	M	E	R	S		D	A	M		T	R	E	K
E	A	U		L	O	D		D	E	B		U	R	I
M	R	S		I	R	E		D	E	E		A	R	E
A	Y	E		N	E	W		A	K	A		H	I	S

Puzzle 46

B	A	K	E		L	A	H	R		H	A	M	A	S
A	L	A	N		A	R	I	A		E	R	I	C	H
G	E	M	S		T	O	M	B		S	M	I	T	E
E	N	E		F	E	D		B	E	T		I	S	M
L	U	N	A	R		E	I	G	E	R				
			B	A	A	L	S		G	R	A	V	E	S
C	L	E	A	N	S	E	S		S	H	E	V	A	
L	O	D		D	A	N		A	R	T		E	E	L
A	B	N	E	R		C	H	A	R	I	S	S	E	
D	E	A	L	E	R		C	A	M	E	L			
		I	S	A	A	C		E	L	A	T	H		
M	A	S		C	Y	D		T	E	T		B	R	O
I	M	N	A	H		A	G	E	D		D	O	E	R
S	M	O	T	E		M	O	V	E		A	D	E	N
T	O	W	E	R		S	T	A	N		M	E	S	S

Puzzle 47

```
.  O  D  E  .  H  A  T  E  D  .  A  R  M  S
S  P  E  D  .  O  L  I  V  E  .  R  O  O  T
H  E  S  S  .  S  T  E  I  N  .  M  A  R  A
A  R  E  .  S  E  A  .  L  I  B  E  R  T  Y
K  A  R  L  M  A  R  X  .  M  A  N  .  .  .
E  S  T  E  E  .  S  I  R  .  D  I  N  A  H
.  .  O  A  K  .  I  I  I  .  A  U  T  O  .
E  T  A  .  R  I  D  .  B  C  E  .  T  E  T
G  A  N  G  .  D  E  B  .  E  N  E  .  .  .
G  U  I  L  T  .  E  E  K  .  J  E  A  N  S
.  .  A  R  K  .  G  O  M  O  R  R  A  H  .
M  A  N  S  I  O  N  .  S  A  Y  .  A  B  A
I  R  A  S  .  R  A  S  H  I  .  A  R  O  D
L  A  M  E  .  A  S  K  E  D  .  N  A  T  E
A  B  E  S  .  H  A  I  R  S  .  N  T  H  .
```

Puzzle 48

```
T  A  L  .  M  B  A  .  D  O  S  .  S  P  A
A  K  A  .  D  O  R  .  E  N  E  .  A  L  S
R  A  M  .  X  X  I  .  B  E  A  .  F  A  N
A  B  B  A  .  I  S  M  .  G  R  E  E  N  E
H  A  S  M  O  N  E  A  N  .  O  R  D  E  R
.  .  H  U  N  G  .  T  A  M  A  R  .  .  .
C  H  A  S  E  .  A  R  M  E  D  .  F  A  A
F  I  N  E  .  A  L  I  E  N  .  K  I  S  S
A  S  K  .  A  R  I  A  S  .  S  A  R  A  H
.  .  S  H  E  A  R  .  P  A  S  S  .  .  .
S  A  R  A  I  .  S  C  H  E  C  H  T  E  R
C  R  O  W  N  S  .  H  A  S  .  A  B  L  E
E  T  A  .  O  O  H  .  N  A  P  .  A  L  E
N  I  S  .  A  N  I  .  D  C  I  .  S  I  D
T  E  T  .  M  G  M  .  S  H  E  .  E  S  S
```

Puzzle 49

B	A	T		H	A	M		R	A	M		N	A	P
E	T	A		E	R	I		E	R	E		A	G	E
A	L	B	E	R	T	S	A	B	I	N		H	A	T
M	I	L	T		S	H	R	E	D		P	U	R	E
S	T	E	A	L		M	E	L		T	A	M	A	R
	M	A	M	A		S	A	H	L					
U	G	H		P	O	S	T		L	E	M	O	N	S
L	E	O	N		S	H	A	K	E		S	A	N	K
T	E	R	E	S	H		L	I	N	E		K	E	Y
	R	H	E	A		N	U	T	S					
P	R	I	D	E		B	A	D		C	H	O	S	E
L	A	D	S		B	U	R	N	T		O	R	A	L
A	G	O		W	E	S	T	E	R	N	W	A	L	L
T	E	L		A	L	E		S	E	E		T	O	I
E	D	S		Y	A	R		S	E	T		E	N	S

Puzzle 50

H	A	M		M	A	T	Z	O		M	O	V	I	E
A	K	A		A	G	A	I	N		A	R	E	N	S
G	A	G		L	O	R	N	E	G	R	E	E	N	E
A	B	I	D	E			G	E	T					
R	A	C	E		S	S	E		M	I	R	I	A	M
	B	A	T	H	E	D		N	I	D	R	E		
E	M	A		B	A	A	L	I	S		D	E	E	D
T	I	S		E	I	K		S	H	E		A	L	A
R	A	I	N		R	E	I	N	E	R		S	I	D
O	M	E	N	S		S	T	E	V	E	N			
G	I	L	E	A	D		S	Y	A		O	M	E	R
	B	A	G				U	N	I	T	E			
T	A	B	E	R	N	A	C	L	E	S		T	H	E
A	H	A	V	A		B	L	O	W	S		L	E	D
S	A	G	E	S		E	I	G	E	R		A	L	S

Puzzle 51

M	A	S	A	D	A	■	B	A	K	E	■	R	A	G
A	T	O	N	E	S	■	R	H	E	A	■	E	R	R
S	E	N	D	A	K	■	O	A	R	S	■	T	I	E
■	■	■	■	L	E	A	■	■	R	E	F	U	S	E
S	H	E	M	■	R	A	B	B	I	■	I	R	A	N
H	O	T	E	L	■	A	R	E	■	A	N	N	I	E
A	R	A	R	A	T	■	O	L	I	V	E	■	■	■
S	A	M	■	B	E	R	N	A	R	D	■	N	O	W
■	■	H	A	L	O	S	■	K	A	D	E	S	H	■
R	I	S	E	N	■	B	O	B	■	T	A	B	L	E
A	S	P	S	■	D	E	N	I	M	■	M	O	O	N
S	H	O	S	H	A	■	■	T	A	P	■	■	■	■
H	U	R	■	E	V	E	S	■	V	A	N	I	S	H
B	A	T	■	L	A	M	P	■	E	L	I	S	H	A
A	H	S	■	P	R	A	Y	■	N	E	P	H	E	W

Puzzle 52

E	T	A	M	■	B	A	B	E	L	■	R	O	B	■
N	E	B	O	■	A	F	U	L	A	■	M	I	N	E
O	V	E	R	■	S	T	R	I	P	■	O	D	E	S
S	A	L	E	■	K	E	N	■	D	R	E	G	S	■
■	■	■	Y	A	I	R	■	B	I	R	D	■	■	■
■	S	H	A	H	N	■	M	O	R	S	E	L	S	■
A	T	O	M	S	■	R	O	N	A	■	C	A	P	P
S	O	T	S	■	R	O	S	E	N	■	A	R	I	A
P	O	E	T	■	A	B	E	S	■	E	I	G	E	R
■	P	L	E	D	G	E	S	■	A	S	K	E	R	■
■	■	■	R	O	S	S	■	P	L	E	A	■	■	■
S	H	E	D	S	■	■	C	O	B	■	P	H	I	L
H	O	R	A	■	W	H	A	L	E	■	L	O	B	E
O	L	A	M	■	N	E	V	E	R	■	A	L	E	F
E	D	S	■	■	W	R	E	S	T	■	N	E	X	T

About the Author

Kathi Handler currently sells Jewish books and a wide range of books on the Internet. She uses her knowledge of Jewish life to offer challenging puzzles and a fine assortment of books. She and her husband reside in Waterbury, Connecticut and own Broder's Rare & Used Books.